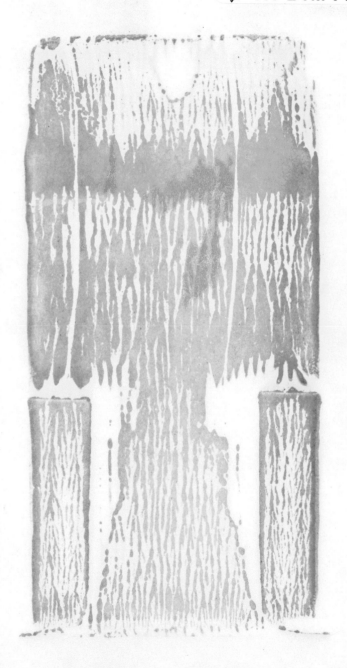

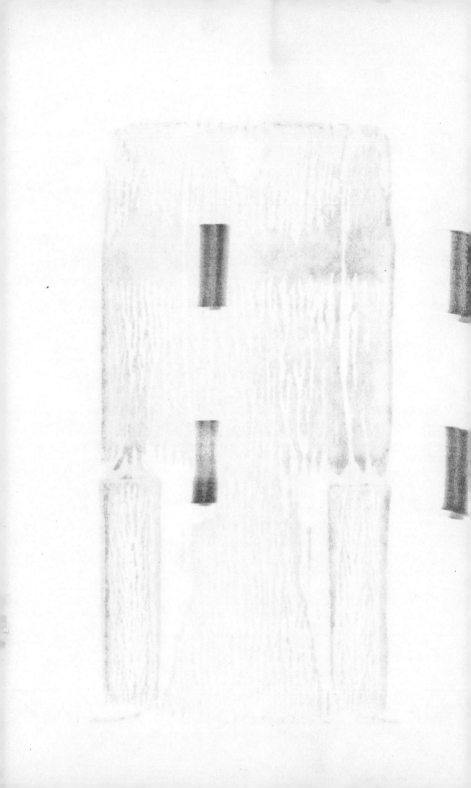

THE
FRENCH
AND
INDIAN
WAR

THE MASSACRE AT FORT WILLIAM HENRY

THE FRENCH AND INDIAN WAR

An informal history

by Donald Barr Chidsey

Illustrated

CROWN PUBLISHERS, INC., NEW YORK

By the Same Author

Contents

THE
FRENCH
AND
INDIAN
WAR

CHAPTER

1

The Tall Virginian

THE TALL VIRGINIAN was twenty-two, and he had not yet learned to control a temper naturally sharp. When he learned by messenger from Half-King, the Seneca chief, that there was a party of about fifty Frenchmen headed his way, he boiled over. He picked some forty men from his force of 150-odd, and with them marched all night through the wilderness to the Indian encampment, where Half-King, who hated the French, verified the report.

This was in Western Pennsylvania or perhaps in Virginia: both colonies claimed the land.[1] It was May 28, 1754, and raining.

Scouts were sent out, and soon returned to relate that the French were indeed camped nearby. They were thirty-three in number, not fifty as first reported. They were crouched beneath some overhanging rocks, trying to keep dry.

The tall Virginian—his name was George Washington, though among the Iroquois he was known as Conotocarious—lost no time. He believed that his force of militia, his first independent command, was about to be attacked; and he meant to get there first. Besides Half-King he took along another chief, Monakatoocha, and a handful of braves. These

11

savages had no firearms, which were in short supply along that part of the frontier, but of course they carried scalping knives. They would not have gone anywhere without their scalping knives.

The Frenchmen, at dawn, were preparing breakfast. It had ceased raining, and they had moved out from under the rocks of what Washington was to call a "bower," but their guns still were stacked there. The Virginians came at them from three sides at once, their muskets banging like doors that are slammed. A few of the Frenchmen tried to get to their weapons, but most either were shot down where they stood or, seeing the Indians in the background, hurriedly surrendered. The Virginians had one man killed, two slightly wounded. Ten Frenchmen dropped, either dead in their tracks or to be killed immediately afterward by the Indians.

The Indians, who had taken no part in the tussle, now swarmed over the field, hacking off scalps.

This was a messy, disgusting process, though mercifully brief. The savage put a foot on the fallen man's face or chest to hold the head steady while he sliced the skin all the way around just underneath the hairline. Then he dropped his knife and seized the hair with both hands. With one great yank, a ripping as of canvas, and a prodigious splashing of blood, he tore the thing off, a trophy for his belt, for the wall of his lodge. It made no difference to him that somebody else had killed the man, or that he wasn't a man at all but a woman or a child, or that he was not even dead at the time. He was usually dead afterward anyway, if only because he had lost so much blood. Occasionally, not often, a wounded person survived a scalping, to wear a wig for the rest of his life; but there was nothing like that near the "bower" of rocks.[2]

Among the dead was the French commanding officer, Joseph Coulon de Villiers, Sieur de Jumonville. He was an ensign, scarcely more than a boy.

THE DEATH OF COULON DE VILLIERS, SIEUR DE JUMONVILLE, ON
MAY 28, 1754

One Frenchman, a private named Mouceau, escaped. He
had stepped into the bushes to answer a call of nature, when
the shooting started. He hared out of there, to make his way
back to his base, Fort Duquesne, with the news.

It had been the tall young Virginian's first action, and he
enjoyed it. "I heard the bullets whistle," he wrote to his
brother Jack, back in Mount Vernon, "and, believe me, there
is something charming in the sound." [3]

He might well be exuberant. He had just started a war,
the first global war; and the stake was a continent.

2

At Daggers Drawn

It COULD BE ARGUED that, when George Washington rushed the de Jumonville group, he did not really precipitate a war but only recognized its existence. This was his own attitude. In the century and a half that England and France had faced each other, snarling, in the New World, peace had never really broken out—except on paper. To all intents and purposes the two nations, in America as in India, were at war all the time.

There had been three formal wars, declared wars, so far. These were, in America—and they were all offshoots of European conflicts—King William's War, 1689–1697; Queen Anne's War, 1702–1713; and King George's War, 1743–1748, though the fighting in between had been frequent. The fourth one, the new one, was to be called by European historians the Seven Years' War, though actually it lasted nine years in America, where it was called the French and Indian War.

The treatment of the Indians from the beginning was a most important difference between the French attitude and that of the English, and this not for reasons of humanity—

14

there was precious little of the humane on either side—but for purely military reasons.

The settlers along the coast—the English in Virginia and New England, the Germans in Pennsylvania, the Dutch in New York, the Swedes in Delaware and New Jersey, the Huguenots of the Carolinas—did not admire the Indian. At first they feared him, understandably; but this feeling was early replaced by one of unmitigated contempt, then by one of peevish annoyance.

The Indians that they met were for the most part contemptible enough. They were not organized, self-reliant savages, but sickly, broken, miserable bodies of men and women with no culture, no traditions worth mentioning, no point-at-able possibilities. They were not dependable, and certainly they weren't clean. They fought among themselves. They tortured their prisoners not for purposes of extracting possibly valuable military information but purely and simply because they liked to witness, and listen to, human agony: in most Indian villages the green-wood slow-burning stake to which the victims were lashed was the accepted public amusement center, the equivalent of a Latin-American plaza or a New England bandstand.

Though many of the early settlers were men of pronounced piety, with very few exceptions they took no interest in the moral well-being of the redskin, being much too concerned with their own state of grace. The Indian indeed was not supposed to have a soul, as human beings did, but rather to be an animal, like the cow, the horse, the pig. Except for trading purposes, and then in the most meager manner possible, nobody ever dreamed of trying to learn any of the Indian languages.

The French, on the other hand, were fascinated by the Indians. They met a better class of them, to start with. Penetrating nearer to the heart of the continent by means of the St. Lawrence, the Great Lakes, the Mississippi, the Missouri, they encountered the Chippewas, the Algonquins, the Cherokees, the Creeks, even the distant Sioux, with all of whom they made friends. They also encountered the Iroquois, the fiercest fighters and cruelest killers of them all, but with these the French did not make friends, though they tried. The Iroquois, a federation that was originally the brainchild of a Mohawk genius named Hiawatha,[4] were organized as the Five Nations, and recently had become the Six Nations. They occupied virtually all the colony of New York, but they had an influence wider than that: the Mohawks, for example, periodically collected tribute from the weak New England tribes as far east as Cape Cod. Iroquois was the French name for these Indians, who were called Maqua by the Dutch, Mingoes by the English, and Mengwee by most of the surrounding tribes. The French had seen them first, and had introduced them to firearms, but in the wrong way.

Samuel Champlain and two companions, the first white men ever to penetrate to those parts, were on the lake that was to be named after him, accompanying a party of Ottawas, when they met a party of Iroquois of comparable size. Naturally there was a battle. The Ottawas persuaded the white men to join the fray, using their muskets, something that Champlain was at first loath to do. The result was spectacular. The Iroquois, proud men, at the sight of all that flash and smoke, the sound of all those explosions, ran away, for they assumed that the gods had intervened against them. When they learned the truth—that they had been tricked—they were furious. They never did forgive the French.

They had no notable fondness for the standoffy English either, but when the two were at daggers drawn, as was usually the case, the Six Nations—the Senecas, Oneidas, Onondagas, Mohawks, Cayugas, and the latecoming Tuscaroras—always, if unenthusiastically, allied themselves to the English. The French spent much time and firewater trying to win them over, or at least to keep them neutral, but in vain.

With all other tribes the French were most amazingly successful at ingratiating themselves. They learned the languages, they respected the customs and adopted the habits, they married the women. So far from striving to "civilize" these savages, they went right along with them in their fondness for surprise attacks, undercover fighting, and prolonged torture. Many of them wore Indian clothes and on occasion painted their faces. The French *coureur de bois* was more than just a man who dealt intimately with Indians: he *was* an Indian, and often even his fellow countrymen could not tell him apart from the savages with whom he surrounded himself. He forgot anything he might ever have known about the storybook aspects of war—the parade-ground precision, unquestionable obedience, gallant be-plumed appearance. He preferred to kill from behind, and he never hesitated to use his scalping knife on a dead or dying man, or to flaunt the grisly trophy afterward.

The French were very much concerned with the immortal soul of the redskin. They sent over Jesuits by the droves, men eager to preach, willing to endure the hardship of months on end in the wilderness, of hunger, and of unspeakable cruelties, men determined to convert the savages, their brothers, at whatever cost. The heroism of these priests has never been outshone; and the Indian was impressed.

English rum was cheaper than French brandy. It was stronger, too. It made you drunk sooner and kept you drunk longer. Still, in another commodity lately introduced into the American-Indian community, gunpowder, the French were decidedly superior. The French produced the best gunpowder in the world.

The simple population figures make patent the French need for friendship with the Indians. At the time of the final, deciding war—*the* French and Indian War itself—the total white population of New France, including Acadia, all of Canada (except a negligible strip around Hudson's Bay, which belonged to England), the Mississippi basin, and Louisiana, was 70,000. And it was stationary. The population of the thirteen Anglo-Saxon seacoast colonies was almost 1,500,000, of whom almost one-fifth were slaves. And it was growing.

The French plunged into the wilderness fearlessly, making astonishing trips of exploration. The English obliterated the wilderness, laying it low as they pushed westward, leaving behind them only stumps.[5]

The French were fond of pointing out that *they* were interested in two things only, souls and furs. They were adventurers, not settlers. When they had made their pile they would go home. "Get rich and get out" was popular advice in New France. The English, however, the French went on, were in America to stay. They were multiplying. They were planting fields, and more fields, which they were prepared to defend. Pretty soon, if this was kept up, there would be no more hunting grounds. The Indian listened, nodding his head.

The French in New France were homogeneous. Not only were they all of the same nationality, they were all of the same religion. Huguenots were not allowed, any more than were foreigners. The government was rotten, but it worked. The governor was supreme under the king, and the line of command was clearly marked. Such things as mutinies or even angry murmurs were inconceivable. Every able-bodied man was in the militia; and if he might be awkward on parade, and nothing much to look at, he was effective in the forest, at guerrilla warfare, *la petite guerre*, or, as the English called it, bushfighting. It was at this, this distinctively American way of fighting, that the French excelled.

The Eastern seaboard colonies were quite different.

There were thirteen of them, and some, like Connecticut and Rhode Island, were virtually self-governing, while others, like Pennsylvania and Maryland, were family-owned. They could not get along with their neighbors. They were cantankerous. Sometimes for a short while a few of them would work together, as did the four that made up New England when in King George's War they assembled to besiege and most valiantly to take the fortress of Louisbourg, "the Dunkirk of America"; but this was a rare exception, and even *it* had ended in a splutter of hard feeling, curses, recriminations. There were thirteen bodies of militia, all of them badly organized, none expert in bushfighting but each rather striving to practice "the art of war" as they conceived it on various village greens, which would have done no good against the Indian or the Frenchman-turned-Indian.

Virginia had an Establishment, and most of the New England colonies (Rhode Island was the exception) were under a highly centralized Congregational Church, but other colonies tolerated all sorts of worshippers, even Quakers, even—in the case of Rhode Island—Jews. This might have been morally laudable, but militarily it was a mistake. Minority groups opposed to war could play hell with appropriations.

The royal governors were appointed by the Crown, but they were not paid by the Crown. They were paid by the various provincial assemblies, which might at any time, when a governor refused to jump to their whistle, withhold his salary, ruining him. Each provincial legislature was a separate entity that did as it pleased, angrily refusing to cooperate with any of the others.

Geography, too, must be considered. There were no roads into the interior, and the thirteen colonies, like Chile, seemed doomed to be irretrievably hemmed in along a thin strip between mountains and the sea, with the French to the north of them and Spaniards to the south, while the west was

thick with French-supplied Indians. If they were to get out
of this—and they were a pushy, dogged lot—the colonists
must find natural passes, the routes taken by the rivers.

New France had the glorious St. Lawrence, which
stretched easily to the Great Lakes, from which in turn it
was but a short portage to the upper reaches of the Mississippi, highway to the Gulf of Mexico. The east-coast colonists enjoyed no such avenue to the hinterland, though they
made the best of what they had, generally establishing cities
at the head of navigation: thus, Richmond is at the falls of
the James, Alexandria at the falls of the Potomac, Trenton at
the falls of the Delaware.

There were some openings, punctuated by portages.
The Hudson River, for instance, forty miles north of Albany
turns sharply to the west, and the traveler who kept going
north from this point had only twelve miles of wilderness
before he reached Lake George, thirty smooth miles of north-
sailing; then, by means of a short river, to Lake Champlain,
twice as large as Lake George and likewise stretching north
and south—out of which flows the Richelieu River into the
St. Lawrence near Montreal. This route, though never a
gateway to the west, was of tremendous importance to both
sides in the struggle for North America. There was the
Mohawk Valley route, by the river of that name due west
from the Hudson a little above Albany, thence over a lake
and a small river to Lake Ontario at a place called by the Indians "Oswego." And there was the Cumberland Gap, named
after the hero of Culloden, roughly where Kentucky, Virginia, and Tennessee now meet.[6]

The kings of France, though they would give governor-
ships to favorites and trade privileges to financial pressure
groups, for the most part looked upon Canada and Louisiana
as one vast personal real estate holding. The kings of England
were more generous, and they gave away immeasurable
tracts of New World land, with a result that conflicting

claims west of the Appalachians were inevitable, and the resolution of such claims was sure to be bloody. Some colonies, like Virginia, only claimed land as far west as the Mississippi, while others, like Connecticut, contended that their grants went all the way to the Pacific, wherever that was.

"Ohio" was the name Virginians gave to that vast territory (which few of them ever had seen) bounded by the Great Lakes to the north, the Ohio River to the south, the Mississippi, and the Alleghenies. Anybody who controlled that territory would cut New France in half, would separate Quebec from New Orleans.

The French of Canada, perceiving this, had taken steps to strengthen the already strong French claims to the territory. They had sent out an expedition which made its way, largely by water, to the so-called Forks of the Ohio, the place where the Allegheny and Monongahela rivers meet to form the Ohio proper, a naturally strong spot that was soon to become famous as the Gibraltar of the Mountains. From there the Frenchmen dropped down the Ohio, stopping every now and then to fasten a lead plate to a tree or to bury one in a shallow, carefully marked grave. These plates proclaimed that all the land everywhere around there —the agents of Louis XV were nothing if not grandiose— belonged forever to the King of France, who forbade it to anybody but his own Catholic subjects.

The Ohio Company of Virginia—composed mostly of Virginians, though there were a few Londoners—had been formed a little earlier, in 1747. It got a grant of 500,000 acres between the Kanawha and the Monongahela rivers, and hoped to establish relations with the Indians there and to divert some of the traffic in furs from the St. Lawrence and Mohawk routes. That Pennsylvania and New France also claimed this territory made no difference to the Virginians.

One of the organizers of the Ohio Company was Lawrence Washington, who soon thereafter died, leaving his shares, and also his estate, Mount Vernon, to his brother George, a major then in the Virginia militia.

There was consternation in those circles when it was learned what the French had done, and Governor Robert Dinwiddie,[7] an acute Scot who was also a stockholder in the Ohio Company, decided to send the broad-shouldered young Washington to tell them that they must not do it.

Here was a hard task, especially in the middle of winter, but Washington did his best. He found the French in several forts, buildings that did not awe him. The French were polite. They took him in, fed him, and told him through an interpreter—Washington never was to learn a word of that language—that he was intruding (oh, no doubt unwittingly!) upon the territory of the King of France. Then everybody bowed, and Washington went back.

The following spring the Ohio Company of Virginia sent a small party west with orders to build a fort at the forks of the Ohio, a site recommended by young Washington. The men had started to do this when from the north there came an overwhelming body of French soldiers who ordered them off. There was no shooting, not even a scuffle. The Virginians left.

To George Washington, a lieutenant colonel now, this was an act of war, and when he was sent at the head of a large body of militia—large, that is, by frontier standards—it was to establish a post at Wills Creek, Fort Cumberland, at the head of navigation on the Potomac, with the understanding that he would soon make his way to the Forks, 122 miles off. As far as *he* was concerned, the two nations already were at war. Where *he* came from, soldiers did not march in set European patterns, but fought as they found things. Nobody in America had ever cried, "*Messieurs le garde français, tirez!*" or ever would. Students might send one another formal challenges; lawyers might; but that was not the way things were done in the wilds.

So—he jumped Jumonville.

3

Dire Necessity

IMPROVISATION WAS THE KEYNOTE of frontier activity. They did with what they had out there. The first forts were no more than sturdily built trading posts, but these soon evolved into the blockhouse, a square log structure of two stories, the upper story sticking far out over the earth. Soon this would be surrounded by a palisade made of the logs of whatever trees were available, logs driven deep into the earth and always sharpened on top. Perhaps, too, a ditch would be dug.

At first these forts were meant only for protection against the weather and perhaps to stave off Indian forays or marauding animals, but soon they came to resemble orthodox European establishments, with curtains, towers, parapets, embrasures, even outworks such as *redans, flèches, demilunes*. It was at this time that the ditches were introduced. They were always called that—ditches—never moats or fosses.

The French were thinking of the English, the English of the French, when they put up these buildings.

Some of these backwoods strongholds were *forts de bois*, dependent upon their stout walls and their palisades; some were *forts de terre*, the walls of which were made up of earth and stone packed into the space between two wooden fences; and a few were combinations. Construction stone was not always available, and none of these forts could have stood up against a real European-style siege with lines of circumvallation and massed batteries of 18-pound guns. It was assumed, when they were first built, that neither side ever would be able to mount such a siege. Sometimes, small brass fieldpieces might be worked up the rivers, across the lakes, over the portages, but never big ones.

The unpretentious fort that the Ohio Company men had started to put up at the Forks was quickly torn down by the Frenchmen who chased them away, and a much stouter structure was erected in its place. They called this Duquesne, after the governor of New France. It was a *fort de bois* on the two water sides, a *fort de terre* on the land side. It was 154 × 160 feet, and strong.

To this haven the soldier Mouceau, the sole French escapee from what was sometimes to be called, sarcastically, the Battle of the Bower, brought his report of the attack of the Virginians under Washington upon Jumonville's party.

The French did not immediately make up a punishment party, for they were expecting reinforcements and they did not wish to weaken too much the garrison at Fort Duquesne. However, that they would strike back, as soon as they were ready, was as sure as the night follows the day. Washington knew this. He gathered about him his scanty force, sent his prisoners down to Wills Creek, and fell back to the Great Meadows, where he built a fort, palavered with the redskins, and wrote many letters to Governor Dinwiddie, who he did not think was supporting him properly.

Great Meadows was not notably great, unless it was compared with the nearby Little Meadows, which was very small indeed. These were almost the only open places for many miles around, where the land, whether flat or hilly— and it was usually hilly—was thick with giant sycamores, oaks, sugar maples, chestnut, pine, cypress. Great Meadows measured 234 acres in a wide valley between Laurel Ridge to the east and Chestnut Ridge to the west. It was between 200 and 300 yards wide and about two miles long. It was marshy in parts, and through it meandered the 10-foot-wide Great Meadows Run.

It was not the best of all possible sites for a stronghold—hills within easy cannon range looked down upon it—but perhaps it was the best that Washington could find without retreating across the mountains. He built there a *fort de bois*, a ramshackle structure of which he seemed disproportionately proud.[8] He called this place Fort Necessity.[9]

Dinwiddie wrote to congratulate him on the early victory and to promise him a medal, his first; but the governor had little to say about Washington's complaint about the officers' pay, nor was he at all specific about the promised reinforcements.

The governor was naturally of an optimistic disposition. He had promised Washington a thousand Indians from the southern colonies, Creeks and Cherokees principally, but none of these ever did appear. The Half-King (this was a sort of title, rather than a name: the *name* of the Seneca chief was Monacathothe, or Tanaghrisson, or perhaps Tanachariston) did show up with about 80 of the more than 200 Indians he had promised, but half of these were women and children and all of them had voracious appetites. The Indians were touchy. They insisted upon getting the same rations as the white men; otherwise they would not stay. This was particularly trying for Washington just then, for his flour and bacon were very low and appeals to the contractors at home only brought still further complaints about the shortage of wagons. An itinerant trader did pass through with a good supply of flour, and Washington bought it all, but he had to pay 21s 8d a hundredweight, which hurt.

Ammunition was getting low, too. Washington kept pleading for more.

It was at this time that he heard of the death of the

GOVERNOR ROBERT DINWIDDIE

ranking officer of the Virginia militia, Colonel Joshua Fry. In the same mail there was a letter from Governor Dinwiddie notifying him that he had been promoted to full colonel. There were no generals in America, and Washington now was the military commander of his colony.

Some reinforcements did arrive, from Georgia, but they were under the command of a well-born young Scot named James Mackay, who held only a captain's commission—but a commission directly from the King. It made all the difference. Such a man could not be expected to take orders from a mere colonial, even though *his* commission had been given him by the governor *as a representative of King George,* and even though the colonial's military rank might be three notches above his own.

As for Washington, if he obeyed a mere captain, even a captain with a King's commission, he could no longer hold the respect of his men.

These two had exquisite manners, and they did not snarl at one another. They were not making fools of themselves, as it might at first seem. This was a serious matter, a knotty problem in a place where there was no superior from whom to ask a decision. They worked it out somehow; but there was an uncomfortable week.

Then came alarming news from Chief Monakatoocha, who was out there somewhere prowling. Washington trusted Monakatoocha. He had, he said by messenger, spent several days either in or near Fort Duquesne, and the French, he had learned, were expecting a large reinforcement. In a matter of no more than days, Monakatoocha warned, a force of about 800 Frenchmen and 400 Indians would be setting forth to strike the Virginians.

It had been Washington's purpose, if ever he got those reinforcements, that ammunition, that flour and bacon, to launch an attack of his own against the fort at the Forks. Now he would be lucky if he could hold on to Necessity. He had fewer than 300 soldiers well and equipped to fight. He ordered trenches dug around the fort outside the palisade, evidently thinking of these as an outer line of defense.

The Indians deserted. They said nothing, made no speeches. They simply faded into the forest, to be seen no more, the Half-King among them. The Virginians had no gifts for them (once again, Washington had been promised gifts but once again they had failed to appear), as the French would have. Besides, the Virginians were sure to lose, and the Indians did not like to be on the losing side. Losers don't get scalps.

The first shot sounded just before dawn on July 3, and a sentry was wounded in the heel. Washington promptly ordered everybody to battle stations, which included the trenches outside. Just at that time, as though answering a signal, the rain started. It did not rain hard at first, but it was persistent, penetrating; the men had all they could do to keep their cartridges dry, and the trenches soon were knee-deep in water.

The firing was sporadic, not steady. Most of the balls were wasted. Seldom was even part of a Frenchman seen, and never parts of an Indian, though the Indians kept up their shrieking. After five or six hours of this the French tried a new tactic. They came out from cover and lined up as though for a formal mass attack. They even fired one volley at an impossible distance, hoping, it must be supposed, that this would frighten the English colonists into surrender. Washington got his men out of the trenches and lined them up in good order, bayonets fixed—those who had bayonets. The French after one look broke ranks, taking to the trees again.

In this they were wise. Why should they risk a mass assault when time already was on their side? They were not in the vast numbers Monakatoocha had foretold, but they were more than the number needed for the task at hand. Their base was only a few miles behind them, the colonists' base was far. The colonists were known to be low in ammunition. Moreover, the ground around Fort Necessity, whether because of neglect or from lack of labor, had not been well cleared; many trees still stood, and the French and their Indian allies took advantage of the cover thus offered. They could fire right over the walls in some places. They aimed not only at men but at all the animals they could see—horses, cows, even dogs.

The rain got worse. It was torrential now, and Washington ordered the trenches evacuated. The men got behind the walls, though these did them little good.

Late in the afternoon, but while it was still light, somebody out there shouted, *"Voulez-vous parler?"* When this was translated to Colonel Washington he replied right away that no, he certainly wouldn't parley. The call came again, however, soon afterward. It was suggested, at the top of somebody's lungs, that the colonists send out two officers who could speak French, and it was promised that they would not be hurt.

Now, there *were* only two officers who could speak French in Fort Necessity, and these were Jacob van Braam, a Dutchman, and William La Peyroney, a Huguenot. Both were captains. Washington sent them forth, and they returned with verbal conditions that Washington scorned. Any order he would even consider, he said, must be in writing.

It was getting dark now, and there was no let-up in the rain.

Van Braam went forth again, to return with a paper on which was written the terms—in French, of course. Washington listened to these, in Van Braam's translation, and still he shook his head. The terms as a whole were unexpectedly generous, but they did demand that all "munitions of war" be turned over to the French. Washington pointed out that this would be simple suicide. If they were to set forth for Wills Creek with no powder in their muskets they wouldn't get a mile before they lost their scalps. Van Braam went forth yet again.

This time he was gone for a long while, and those inside the fort feared that the Indians had got him and were burning him alive; but at last he returned, soaked to the skin, and on the paper he clutched, sure enough, the words "munitions de guerre" had been scratched out.

Washington asked that the whole thing be read over to him again, and this was a job for Van Braam alone, since La Peyroney either was ill or had been wounded.

The paper was wet, the ink had run, and it had been

badly written in the first place—no doubt living conditions among the attackers were unpleasant too. Van Braam had only the stump of one candle. Moreover, though his French was good enough, his English was limited. He translated from French into Dutch in his mind, and then put that into English, *his* English.

The French explained that they had no thought of provoking hostilities against their English neighbors but only wished to drive those responsible for the "assassination" of the Sieur de Jumonville back to their own side of the mountains. The prisoners taken on that occasion must be returned, and two officers must be given as hostages *for* their return. The colonists could keep anything they could carry on their backs, all the horses being dead. They could march out with honors of war.

It seemed all right.

It was indeed better than might have been hoped for. Washington signed. So did Captain Mackay, who of course could not have a mere colonial officer answer for the capitulation of his own men. But Mackay had not been present at the attack upon de Jumonville's party; and Washington had. Mackay then did not in effect sign a confession of murder. Washington did.

Van Braam, whether from ignorance or a desire to get the damned business over with, had not translated the word *assassinat* as "assassination" but only as something rather less—perhaps "death" or even "killing" (nobody could be quite sure afterward), but definitely not "assassination."

But that's what Washington signed, though he did not know it at the time. Learning about it later was to prove a humiliating experience. The French published that paper and made propaganda of it. Europe was shocked, and so indeed was George Washington.

Next morning—it was July 4—Washington and his men duly left the premises, to stagger, half-alive, toward Wills

Creek. The flags were flying, the drums were beaten, but nobody could deny that it was an appallingly poor way to open a military career. No matter what excuses might be offered, the fact remained that the Union Jack no longer flew anywhere west of the Alleghenies.

At least, the rain had stopped.

4

The Man for the Job

T HE ALLEGHENIES, a high-spined ridge, a divide, made an excellent natural boundary between the west and the seacoast colonies; but the Alleghenies did not stretch across western New York, which was Iroquois country.

The Iroquois were a dying race, and they knew it, or at least their sachems knew it. Their hunting grounds were largely gone, nibbled away by the white man, and they had perforce succumbed to agriculture. Yet they were many, and a great deal of the old ferocity still was there.

In the all-important fur trade they were middlemen rather than producers. They let the pelts pass through their territory, and especially down the long Mohawk Valley, for a price. The French were constantly intruding upon them from the west and north, the English from the east and south, and the Iroquois—not very successfully, for they had no flair for this kind of thing—tried to play one off against the other, collecting at both ends. Still nominally allied to the English, for they acknowledged George II to be their Great White Chief, they were listening more and more to the wily French who, for their part, viewed with alarm the gradual filtering of the fur trade into Iroquois country through the activities of the Dutch and the English, and away from the St. Lawrence country, which was stringently French.

The situation was made even more complex by the fact that the Iroquois, after their recent smashing victory over the Hurons, claimed the land north of the Ohio all the way to the Mississippi, the very land over which the French and British were about to go to war.

At the same time that George Washington in the wilds of western Pennsylvania was losing the first round of that fight to the French, a congress of responsible representatives of sundry seacoast colonies was considering the question in Albany, New York. There was nothing rebellious about this meeting. On the contrary, its secondary aim, after the conciliation of the complaining Iroquois, was to bring the colonies closer together in order that they might by this means be closer at the same time to the mother country. The congress, indeed, was sponsored by the Board of Trade in London. It had been half a year in preparation, and invitations had been sent out to all the colonies except the three southernmost ones, the Carolinas and Georgia, which had no interest in the Iroquois or in the fur trade. Virginia, always a loner, and very much concerned with her own frontier just at that time, ignored the invitation, as did New Jersey, which had no frontier and was not threatened by redskins. Rhode Island and Connecticut had appointed delegates even before they could be invited.

The final line-up consisted of five from New York, five from Massachusetts, four from New Hampshire, three from Connecticut, two from Rhode Island, two from Maryland, and four from Pennsylvania. The presiding officer was Governor James De Lancey of New York.

The Indians came with dragging feet, most of them deliberately late in order to show that they didn't think much of this powwow, a bad sign at the very start. Gifts were distributed—gifts with which the Indians, as usual, found fault. A committee had framed an elaborate speech for Governor De Lancey, a sort of convention key-note address, and he delivered it with flourishes and at great length. The Indians listened impassively and in silence, but this was not in itself an encouraging circumstance, for they loved long speeches delivered in a florid manner, even though few of them knew English.

The most conspicuous person there, of either race, was William Johnson, who came from County Meath, Ireland, as agent for his uncle, Admiral Sir Peter Warren, who had a large land grant in upper New York.

Johnson was forty years old, big, breezy, red of face, blue of eye. He was a sort of white chief among the members of the Six Nations, the Iroquois, and his house on the Mohawk about 25 miles west of Schenectady was the scene of many tribal councils.[10] He spoke Mohawk, was married to a Mohawk. For all his size, he could do a brilliant war dance when the occasion called for one.

William Johnson did not accomplish much at the congress itself, but it is likely that many of the Iroquois would not have come in the first place had it not been for his arguments.

Sundry sachems made ritual answers to Governor De Lancey, and they were not remarkably polite about it. In particular Tiyanoga, known among the whites as Hendricks, pulled no punches. Why should the warriors of the Six Nations continue to follow the King of England? he asked. The French, he pointed out, protected themselves and their red allies with forts. Did the English? No. Hendricks urged them to do so, if they wished the adherence of his people. He was blunt about it, even bitter.

More gifts were distributed, and deprecated. There was further feasting. And at last, a few days after the fall of Fort

Necessity, about which nobody at Albany had heard, the powwow was dissolved.

Nothing had been accomplished, as far as the Indians were concerned. They had listlessly reaffirmed their devotion to King George, but in truth they were no closer to the English than before, no further from France, and what they would do when war broke out was anybody's guess.

The only *specific* agreement struck at Albany was one between the Pennsylvania delegates and certain Iroquois elders, the legality of which was questionable. By it the Indians made over to the colony of Pennsylvania, for 2,000 eight-pieces, a vast but unspecified territory that would have put the colony on the shores of Lake Erie, also on those of the Ohio River. But France claimed all that territory anyway, and this was an issue that could only be settled by war.

Meanwhile, and apart from all the presentations, the toasts, the speech-making, the drum-thumping, a little group of serious delegates was trying to come up with some plan for central government of the seacoast colonies, or at least central military control. On the second day of the sessions the congress had appointed a committee to study this problem and to report, and it was a good committee: Theodore Atkinson of New Hampshire, Thomas Hutchinson of Massachusetts, Stephen Hopkins of Rhode Island, William Pitkin of Connecticut, William Smith of New York, Benjamin Franklin of Pennsylvania, and Benjamin Tasker of Maryland.

Franklin, the Philadelphia printer, if not the most eminent of these, had done the most thinking on this subject. The colonies were growing in population at a much higher rate than was the mother country, he more than once had pointed out, and soon they would equal or even surpass the mother country. They should be governed the same way, whatever that way was. Franklin envisioned the colonies and the home country as two parts of the same land, and they should be equal in every respect. This could not happen if the colonists continually quarreled among themselves. The French, in such a case, could take them over one by one, or at the best could keep them hemmed in east of the mountains, denying them expansion. Franklin felt very strongly about this. He had recently published a cartoon—it might have been the first political cartoon in America [11]—depicting a snake chopped into eight parts, labeled New England, New York, New Jersey, Pennsylvania, Maryland, Virginia, North Carolina, and South Carolina, with the caption: "Join or Die."

Other delegates besides Franklin had come to the congress with plans for a union of the colonies, but his, the best thought-out, was the only one seriously considered. It provided for a central military fund, a military governor appointed by and paid by the Crown. The special committee, after making a few minor changes, recommended it to the congress as a whole, which in turn recommended it to the various colonies, including those not represented at Albany. Some of the colonies rejected it after brief debate; others did not so much as consider it. Even Pennsylvania turned it down, the Assembly voting against it when Benjamin Franklin happened to be absent. The truth is, the colonies just were not ready for such legislation.

Since the colonies themselves had voted it down, the plan never went to the British government, which in any event probably would have vetoed it, finding that it smelled too much of independence.

News of the disaster beyond the mountains, of the failure of New York, among other colonies, to reinforce Washington as promised, brought about a sober reassessment of the situation. In the conflict to come—and nobody doubted now that it would come *soon*—the French would have a great advantage in position; and if the colonies could not do any better than they had just done to protect themselves, then professional help from home must be sent—a military commander-in-chief capable of pulling them together, of teaching them how to fight.

The British Army was called upon.

A corrupt government usually means a weak army, and that was the case here. The great Whig families—the Pelhams, the Cavendishes, the Lennoxes, the Conways, the Bedfords (sometimes called the Bloomsbury Gang), the Wentworths, Fitzroys, Grenvilles—had been misruling Great Britain for a long time. The regular standing army was unpopular, as always—it was so expensive. Now it had glitter, but not much more. Commissions were bought and sold. Most of the officers were English, but most of the men came from Ireland or (since the Stuart uprising of 1745–1746) from Scotland, in either event being driven to it by poverty; and where there were English privates they were jail scrapings. Inspired leadership was lacking. The days of Monk and Marlborough were but memories, and Wellington had not been born. Who, then, would perform this prodigy of leading an army to America, pulling the colonies together, and wresting a continent from the French?

The person to answer this question was William Augustus, Duke of Cumberland, Knight of the Order of St. George, son of the King, and sometimes called, because of his ruthless stamping out of the Young Pretender's army after Culloden, Billy the Butcher.

Ruthlessness indeed was a fixed policy of young Cumberland, a way of life. His father, unlike *his* father, George I, had learned to speak English, but he spoke it with a heavy German accent, and his heart always was in Hanover. The son too was Germanic in his outlook. He was fussy about all details of uniform, all details of drill. He was exacting. What he might have lacked in insight he made up in energy. Thick, a bulldog in appearance, he had no imagination but a great deal of brute courage. He had made a career of the army, for, like his father, who seldom had time, he loved to play soldier. He was, at this moment, still in his lower thirties, captain-general of all the British land forces. He would pick the man for America.

It must not be supposed for an instant that His Royal Highness would condescend to go to the colonies in person. Nobody ever dreamed of such a thing. But he did know his generals, and he rummaged about among them and came up with one who was not notably well born, not well connected, and not even rich, but who was, like his sponsor, every inch the bulldog—Major General Edward Braddock of the Coldstream Guards.

5

Slaughter on the Monongahela

IT IS A TEMPTATION to style Braddock an early Blimp. Historians have not been kind to him. His was a job that called for genius, which he did not have, but in fact he was no ineffectual fuddy-duddy. His record might not have been brilliant, but it was impeccable. He knew his business. If he was not an innovator, neither was he a fool. It has been said of him, sneeringly, that his military experience was largely confined to the parade ground and the desk, and that he had heard very few shots fired in anger; and this is true, but it was true through no fault of his own, and, as the event was to prove, when he did go into combat it was without a trace of fear.

Two regiments of the line, the 44th and the 48th, were assigned to his command. These had been stationed in Ireland and they were only at about half strength, as was customary in peace times, about 350 each. They were "fleshed out" from English regiments until they numbered about 500 each, and they sailed from Ireland in January of 1755, heading for Hampton Roads, Virginia.

These were not crack regiments—both had panicked at Prestonpans—but they *were* British regulars, and as such

MAJOR GENERAL EDWARD BRADDOCK

were believed to be infallible. They were supposed to enlist about 200 more men apiece in the colonies and to cause *them* to become infallible as soon as possible. When everything was ready they would set forth for the Forks of the Ohio, where Fort Duquesne undoubtedly would fall to their arms.

Professionalism was rampant among the civilians. Soldiers who had been trained in "the art of war" were looked upon as superior persons, creatures from another world, who were possessed of a special magic which they could not or would not impart to mere mortals. This feeling was especially strong in Virginia, where real soldiers never before had been seen, or at least not since 1677, almost a century before, when a mixed battalion of the 1st and the Coldstreams helped to suppress a rebellion. There had been from time to time drills by various so-called Independent Companies, which were supposed to be an integral part of the British Army but in fact were nothing more than uniformed militiamen; but these never had been anything like this. People came from many miles around to the camp Braddock established near Alexandria, to gawp, owl-eyed, at the pipe-clayed belts, the bugles, the flags, the bayonets, and those brilliant red coats. Sir Edmund Andros, when he crossed the sea to take over his duties as governor of the Massachusetts Bay Colony in 1686, had brought with him as honor guard a company of redcoats, and Boston had never liked them, even that long ago. Virginia loved them, to look at.

Virginians showed no hankering to wear that coat that was soon to be spread all over the world. Enlistments were thin. Some Virginians, fewer Marylanders, might consent to serve with their own kind under their own officers in militia groups, but they shied away from the pomp, the iron discipline, the low pay, and bad food of the British Army proper.

The general, the first ever seen in America, had landed February 20, and he was infuriated by what he found. Nothing, it seemed, had been done. A thick-set red-faced man nearing sixty, he had a tendency to bark. When he did not like a thing, which was often, he said so in no uncertain tones. The lack of enlistments enraged him, and when he issued a call for 1,500 horses and 125 wagons and got virtually none he all but burst a blood vessel.

He summoned the governors of Virginia, Maryland, Massachusetts, New York, and Pennsylvania, who met with him at Alexandria. They were loud with promises. It was a bigger step toward union than had been the conference at Albany the previous summer.

Many personages called upon the general—everybody wanted to meet him—but the two who impressed him most were George Washington and Benjamin Franklin.

Washington was in a dilemma. By the new regulations concerning colonial officers, he could not serve in the regular army as anything more than a captain, and of course he could not consider this after having been a colonel. At the same time, he didn't want to lose this opportunity "to study the art of war," as he put it in a letter to General Braddock, "under so illustrious a master." What he proposed, at last, was that he be permitted to serve on the general's staff as a gentleman volunteer with no rank—and without pay. This was agreeable to Braddock, who thus got, for nothing, an advisor who knew the country as well as any man, far better than most, and who in addition was well connected in Virginia, the most important colony from Braddock's point of view, since it was to serve as his base.

Washington thereafter was to have an honored place in General Braddock's "family," or staff, and was always addressed as "Colonel," and always asked to attend councils of war in that capacity. He and the general got to be good friends.

Benjamin Franklin came, ostensibly, to offer his services as a transportation expert, which assuredly he was. He was deputy postmaster general of the colonies, which means that he did all the work, the postmaster generalship itself being a sinecure. In this capacity the plump Philadelphian was able to be of great assistance to the general.

The rates were high: General Braddock was outraged by all the prices he had to pay in America. A wagon and four horses together with the services of a driver cost 15 shillings a day; a horse alone cost two. But horses and wagons were there when Braddock needed them, thanks to Franklin. Braddock had to pay for these out of his own war chest. He had to pay for many things he thought the colonies themselves should have paid for. The governors unanimously had told him that they would not submit to their assemblies any plan for a central fund to which each would contribute;

such a move, they insisted, would be political suicide.

Franklin's *real* purpose was to get the general to shift his base of operations from Virginia to Pennsylvania, which would be good for business, Philadelphia business. The route straight west from Philadelphia to the Forks would be longer, but it would be flatter, and more open, and it contained many more farms and horses than the northwestern route from Alexandria up through the valley of the Potomac. There was ample pasturage along much of the Pennsylvania route, none at all along the Cumberland-Duquesne route, where Braddock would have to carry all his own fodder.[12]

Braddock, however, had politics to think about. Virginia, with its Established Church and its landed proprietors, looked to him like a much safer base than the bustling Quaker-ridden Pennsylvania. He would stick to Virginia.

Braddock liked Franklin, who did not reciprocate.

At one point in the conversation Franklin expressed the belief that the expedition should get to the Forks all right *provided* that care was taken to avoid Indian ambuscades. The Indians, he remarked, had their own way of fighting.

"He smil'd at my ignorance," Franklin later wrote, "and reply'd, 'These savages may, indeed, be a formidable enemy to your raw American militia, but upon the king's regular and disciplin'd troops, sir, it is impossible they should make any impression.' I was conscious of an impropriety in my disputing with a military man in matters of his profession, and said no more." [13]

In addition to the expedition to Fort Duquesne, which he would lead in person, Braddock, as ordered, arranged for two other strikes at French strongholds. He did this through various governors and the military advisors they brought with them.

William Johnson, the jovial Irishman with the Mohawk wife, who had the militia rank of colonel though he lacked any formal military training, was created a major general and authorized to raise some 3,000 men for one campaign only, together with as many Iroquois as he could induce to go along. With these he was to attack and take the French fort at Crown Point, at the head of Lake Champlain, thus sealing off the direct Quebec–New York water route, the invasion route.

William Shirley, governor of the Massachusetts Bay Colony, was a man of spirit and enterprise. Now he proposed to lead a large body of militia, mostly Massachusetts men, to Fort Niagara on Lake Ontario. This would cut the St. Lawrence–Ohio line. Shirley had never served a day in any sort of military outfit, but he too was made a major general.

All three of these great movements were to take place in the summer of 1755.

General Braddock was told by some that if he concentrated his forces in northern New York he could take the Lake George–Lake Champlain–Richelieu River route to Quebec. This was known as "striking at the root." With Quebec captured, it was pointed out, the rest of New France would soon fall, and the other two expeditions would not be necessary. Braddock, however, scorned such advice from amateurs. He had his orders and, by God, he meant to obey them.

Fort Cumberland, the taking-off place, where Wills Creek slithers into the Potomac, was a dreary spot. Spring comes late in those high lands, and at least until the end of April Braddock's most implacable foe was General Mud. There were other reasons for delay. The army did not get moving until June 7.

The distance from Cumberland to the Forks was 112 miles, but it was the thickest sort of wilderness and very rocky. Through this, in as straight a line as possible, Braddock proposed to build a road twelve feet wide. The way had been blazed for them by their advance party.

He had slightly more than 2,000 men in all. The van,

Braddock's March

in command of Colonel Thomas Gage,[14] consisted of 300 regulars. Then there were a small body of guides and a company of grenadiers, the road-making party of army laborers, and a force of 200 Virginian light horse, and, 150 yards back, the main body of 700 soldiers. The general's guard was made up of 50 picked men, and there was a rear guard of 100 Virginians. There were in addition 200 flankers on either side, and there were 30-odd sailors lent to Braddock by Admiral Keppel in order to handle the block-and-tackle operations connected with getting the big stuff over the ridges.[15]

There were only eight Indians. Except in the Iroquois country, it was getting harder than ever for the English to enlist Indians.[16]

From Gage's front to the tail of the rear guard was about 1,900 yards.

Progress was agonizingly slow. At one time they averaged only three miles a day. The wagons were always getting mired, or else they suffered from broken wheels or split axles, but it was the heavy guns that gave the most trouble. At last Braddock called a council, which decided to send back two of the 6-pounders, weighing between 1,300 and 1,500 pounds each, exclusive of their carriages, ammunition, and ball. They still had left four howitzers, four 12-pounders, and two 6-pounders.

The spirit of the men was good. They had faith in their general. Their chief fear was that they would not get a chance to fight, that their slow approach would be reported by Indian scouts, and the French would blow up Fort Duquesne before they could get there.

Yet they saw no scouts. They did not even see the sky most of the time, for the trees were thick and glades were rare. They never saw a shadow move, never heard a leaf rustle. Now and then, especially in the rear guard, a man would step aside for natural purposes—and never return.

COLONEL THOMAS GAGE

Sometimes such a man was found without his hair, and at other times he was not found at all. Even members of the flanking parties, which were always kept out, never glimpsed any sign of a spy.

It was eerie.

The men did not stack their muskets at night but kept them by their sides, loaded. The usual number of sentries was doubled.

Another council decided—with young Colonel Washington strongly urging this—that the force should be split for purposes of speed. A strong advance guard with six cannons, four howitzers, and only thirty-four wagons would be commanded by General Braddock himself, while the sick and a small guard for the heavy supplies, under Colonel Thomas Dunbar, would slog along as best they could. Colonel Washington, suffering from the bloody flux, remained in sick bay, but only after he had obtained Braddock's promise to send for him when the advance guard neared the fort.

The confrontation took place early in the afternoon of July 8, to the amazement of both sides.

Contrecœur, the commander at Fort Duquesne, an elderly, gallant man, did not know whether to vacate the place and blow it up, make a token defense, or send out an intercepting party and pray for a miracle. By means of his Indian scouts he had followed the British advance, and he knew exactly how many men and how many guns Braddock had. Those scouts were all in or around the fort, now that Braddock was near. Contrecœur did not know *how* near. On the morning of July 8 he supposed the British to be still well on the other side of a pair of sharp curves in the Monongahela River. That would be an ideal place to ambush them, it was pointed out to Contrecœur by his second-in-command, Captain Beaujeu.

Daniel Hyacinth Mary Lienard de Beaujeu was the kind of officer that could only be found in New France. He mixed with the Indians, talked their language, played their games. He was an aristocrat, but the only mark of his military rank was the black tricorn he wore on his head and the silver gorget he wore around his neck. Otherwise, in apparel, he was all redskin.

Contrecœur consenting, Beaujeu harangued the Indians, some 800 of them, mostly Ojibways and Ottawas, all reluctant to move out from the comparative safety of the fort. Would they not follow him, their friend? Would they stay at home with the squaws when there was fighting to be done? They did not stir; and he supposed that he had failed; but when with a dramatic gesture he stalked out of the fort, in the company of only 108 regulars and 146 militiamen, a large part of the Indian crowd, some 600 of them, rose and followed.

Before they could reach the nearer curve of the Monongahela, less than ten miles from the fort, in a part of the forest comparatively parklike, they came upon the British.

Braddock's eight Indian scouts had deserted, but he had somehow acquainted himself with the nature of the country just ahead. He knew that the bends of the Monongahela and the space between them would make a perfect spot for an ambush, and he took extraordinary precautions as he approached them.

The river at this point was only 200 yards wide, and it was shallow.

The crossings were made carefully and without incident. No sound broke the silence ahead, the silence on either side.

Once over the second bend and on solid ground again the members of the advance guard naturally relaxed a little. It seemed certain, now, that the French had evacuated Duquesne. At any moment they might hear explosions as the fort was blown up. Officers were making bets among themselves as to when this would happen.

The trees thinned a bit, so that there were spaces where you could have driven a carriage, much more open than anything they had yet encountered on this long, arduous march, this triumph of military engineering, military organization.

Across this semi-open space there straggled a lot of Indians, who stopped short at the sight of the redcoats, who had stopped short at the sight of *them*, the first men they had seen in more than a month.

At the head of the savages was a man who wore a black tricorn with a French cockade, at his breast a silver gorget that doubtless proclaimed his name, his rank, his regimental designation. Otherwise this man was dressed as an Indian, though he was certainly white. He took off his hat, whirled it several times over his head, and shouted something. The real Indians disappeared behind trees, back of bushes, and started to shoot.

The redcoats of the advance guard deployed as best they could in that limited space, and they fired a volley at the blobs of smoke.

Daniel Hyacinth Mary Lienard de Beaujeu fell, but his second-in-command, a Captain Dumas, thought fast. There

BEAUJEU "TOOK OFF HIS HAT, WHIRLED IT SEVERAL TIMES OVER HIS
HEAD, AND SHOUTED SOMETHING."

was a leafy depression to right and left of the British advance
guard, and he ordered the men into these natural entrenchments. This was just luck, since the position had not been
picked, but it was luck that Dumas was quick to take advantage of.

The advance guard contained a few light fieldpieces,
and these were wheeled forward and fired several times into
the forest. Instantly the Canadian militiamen broke and ran,
even the officers. The Ottawas and Ojibways wavered, for

they did not like cannon fire, but the French officers managed to keep them in their places—and to keep them firing.

The British soldiers had not been taught to aim at anything—there was no rear sight on their weapon, the Brown Bess musket—but only to point the muzzle in the general direction of the enemy and fire at command. This they did, again and again.

The Frenchmen and the Indians, on the other hand, made every shot count. They had beautiful targets. The Britishers, crowded together, had not been taught to reload in a kneeling position, much less lying down, and they stood erect in their bright red coats. They fell fast, and their officers even faster.

The flanking parties came crowding in, to find out what was happening. The rear of the van pushed forward, for the same purpose. There was hardly room for a man to move.

George Washington, in such pain that he could hardly stay in the saddle, was here, there, and everywhere. He had two horses shot from under him, and his coat was ripped by balls in several places, but his skin never was nicked. He probably enjoyed every minute of it.

General Braddock, bellowing, sword in fist, tried his damnedest to keep up the fight, but he too made an irresistible target. He had four horses killed under him, and soon after he had mounted the fifth he was himself shot out of saddle. He had got it through the right arm and into the lungs. "Who would have thought of it?" he kept muttering as they carried him to the rear.

There was a hill to the right of the British position which, if seized, might serve as a place from which to sally, widening the action. Captain Thomas Waggener of the Virginians was quick to notice this. He and his men were fighting well, from a prone or kneeling position whenever possible. They were less confused than the redcoats, who never did recover from the first shock of amazement. Waggener gathered as many as he could and started to lead them toward that hill. Soon they learned that they were being fired upon from behind. Either the redcoats mistook them for Indians by reason of their trick of jumping from tree to tree, from bush to bush, or else they had lost their heads entirely. Waggener and his men got back to the crowded place lest they be killed, and by the time they were ready for another try at that hill the French had mounted it with Indians.

Even so, and even though they were not crack troops,[17] the redcoats kept firing, and falling, for more than two hours. Then "they broke and run as Sheep pursued by dogs, and it was impossible to rally them." [18]

They left behind them all the wagons, all the fieldpieces, all Braddock's papers, £25,000 in specie, and large numbers of dead and dying.

Many of the men, lost to all shame, ran. They might have saved themselves the trouble. The French, good soldiers, almost certainly would have pursued the retreaters, taking advantage of their fright and confusion; but the Indians would have no part of such pursuit. With scalps to be taken all over the place, with dead and moaning by the score, the Ottawas and Ojibways could not be herded across the Monongahela.

The Indians and the French lost a mere handful. The British lost, killed and wounded, 977 out of 1,459. Of the 89 British officers involved, only 26 emerged unscathed.

"Who would have thought of it?" General Braddock kept muttering. He died the next night and was buried in an unmarked grave at the edge of the Great Meadow, where a little earlier Washington's Fort Necessity had stood. He was a brave man.

Colonel Dunbar, who succeeded to the command, in a camp near Mount Laurel, almost fifty miles behind the scene of the battle, burned or buried most of his supplies and made

THE DEATH OF GENERAL BRADDOCK

full-speed back to Fort Cumberland. He paused there only for a little while, then took his two regiments of regulars to Philadelphia, where he decided to go into winter quarters—in August.

Still no British flag flew west of the mountains, and the passes all were open.

6

Creation of a Baronet

WILLIAM SHIRLEY, governor of Massachusetts, had been a lawyer by profession, but at heart he was a soldier, a man who craved glory in the field, who even in the middle of the eighteenth century, that time of grandiose military ideas, was outstanding because of his martial ambitions. He had been instrumental in promoting the siege of Louisbourg in 1745, but that was paper labor, and what he longed for was to wave a sword in battle. As a reward for his activity in the Louisbourg affair he had been given a regiment, named after him, of Independent Companies. Now he was to be no longer merely a colonel but a major general. The troops under him were, in effect and often in fact, raw militia; but it was exciting all the same.

At the Alexandria conference with General Braddock, a conference Governor Shirley had attended in considerable state, for he was by no means unaware of his own talents, he had voted enthusiastically, as had the others, for the construction of a British fleet in Lake Ontario.

Why this had not been done earlier it is hard to say. England, like the Scandinavian countries, like the Netherlands, was exceedingly *sea-minded*. In ordinary circumstances she thought first of the water, only later of the land. She had not so acted in the case of the Great Lakes.

The westernmost point of penetration on the part of the British was Oswego, a trading-post-turned-fort at the mouth of the Oswego River, which emptied into Lake Ontario. This had been kept up for many years, but not well. It was a palisaded place in a poor location, falling apart, with only a weak garrison. Why the French had not gulped it, without waiting for a declaration of war, is hard to understand. No doubt it was high on their list of desirable prizes once a real war *did* break out.

Fort Oswego, miserable as it was, was a factor in diverting a good part of the fur trade down the Mohawk Valley instead of down the St. Lawrence.

Fifty watery miles from Oswego, on the northeastern shore of the lake, stood Fort Frontenac, a French establishment, made of native stone but still not strong, and not heavily garrisoned. One hundred and twenty-five miles to the west was Fort Niagara, also French, which itself was 200 miles north and slightly east of Fort Duquesne. If Niagara fell Duquesne must wither on the vine. If Frontenac fell both Duquesne *and* Niagara would wither on the vine. Either way, at least a few gunboats would be needed. The French already had built some.

The plan expounded at Alexandria was that Shirley should lead his militiamen up the Mohawk and across to Oswego, where he would build several lake schooners, equipping these with guns. Then he would descend upon Fort Niagara. By that time, it was assumed, Braddock would have taken Fort Duquesne and would be free to move upon Niagara, which would surely fall before his and Shirley's combined forces, plus the schooners.

They would then, in what was left of the season, besiege and take Fort Frontenac, thus gaining complete control of Lake Ontario and cutting the Quebec-Ohio line. Montreal and Quebec could wait until the following summer.

Even if Braddock had taken Duquesne, this part of the plan probably would have fallen through. Shirley had about 2,500 militiamen, most of them from Massachusetts, a few from New Jersey; but not many of these had known any experience with boats. He made Albany his base, 160 miles from Oswego, and the way largely upstream, with several portages. It took the men almost a month, the provisions much longer. Men without provisions tend to act mutinous, and Shirley had a hard time keeping things quiet.

The fort they found in pitiful condition: it would have fallen at a touch. Shirley feared that if he left it that way and struck at Fort Niagara, the Frenchmen at Fort Frontenac would knock out Oswego in his absence, cutting him off from his base. So he settled down to strengthen Oswego as best he could.

When news of the Braddock disaster came to far-out Oswego, Shirley knew that if he took Niagara he would have to do it alone. Also, the report had it that all General Braddock's papers had fallen to the enemy, who would in this way learn of Shirley's designs against Niagara and Frontenac, spots they would then assuredly strengthen.

What with one thing and another, the energetic Governor Shirley by October was obliged to admit that the whole campaign had been wasted. He left 700 men at the slightly strengthened but still vulnerable Fort Oswego and went back to Massachusetts.

The thrust at Crown Point was more exciting, though not more successful.

The French ministry of war, long before it learned of Braddock's plans, had decided that, while the death of de Jumonville was deplorable, it was not a *casus belli*. Nevertheless it would be well, it was decided, to bolster the French forces in the New World, and with this purpose in mind almost 4,000 regulars were embarked upon ships destined for Quebec. The British Navy, despite epical efforts, managed to cut out only two of the transports, holding about 500 men. The rest got through, crack troops all.

In command of this formidable outfit was Lieutenant General Baron (or Count) [19] Ludwig August von Dieskau. He was very highly thought of, for he had served under the great Marshal Saxe. It is evidence of the seriousness with which the French court was taking this undeclared war across the sea that it sent such a man.

Dieskau established himself at Crown Point, near the upper end of Lake Champlain. He examined a place a little higher up on the lake, also on the west shore, called by the Indians Ticonderoga, but though he approved this as a site for a fort, a stronger place naturally than Crown Point, he did not start to fortify it. He had with him almost 800 regulars, 1,200 Canadian militiamen, and more than 600 Indians. When he left Crown Point September 4 to meet the colonials he took with him only 200 of the regulars, and 680 of the Canadians, but all of the Indians. He had heard through scouts that the Americans were up to something near the head of Lac St. Sacrement, and he meant to find out what it was.

William Johnson had gathered around him at Albany, which was also Shirley's base—the two often conferred at this time, but both were glory grabbers and inevitably they were to fall out—a little more than 3,500 militiamen. All would be new to combat and were unused to any sort of discipline. Only one company, a swank city outfit, was in uniform. Most had brought their own muskets. This was, in short, a typical thrown-together American army—temporary, without traditions, tough, and unpredictable.

Johnson had only a few hundred Indians, despite his own influence over them. These were led by the redoubtable Tiyanoga ("Old Hendricks"). His second-in-command was

Phineas Lyman, a Hartford, Connecticut, lawyer, like Johnson himself without a day's orthodox military training.

They carried an enormous artillery train, for a force that size: six 18-pounders, two 32-pounders, two 8-inch mortars, and one 13-inch mortar, a monstrosity. Pound for pound this was twice as much as Braddock had carried, and Braddock had a great deal of trouble with his, for it formed the chief reason for his slowness. Johnson had no trouble with his artillery despite its siegelike size. The reason for this was the difference in terrain. Braddock had been faced with angry stone ridges, a forbidding forest. Johnson's way was all flat, and most of it was over water.

At the great bend of the Hudson, about forty miles above Albany, he quit that river to strike out for the upper reaches of the long north-south lake called by the French Lac St. Sacrement, which no Englishman ever had seen, though they had heard about it. To guard the portage he left a force of about 500 with orders to build a fort, which was to be called Fort Edward.

They came upon the lake, a thing of beauty, a fairyland, untouched by human hands, the sky above it unblotched by smoke. They were entranced. Johnson, though he had no more title to this body of water than did the French, and indeed not as much, changed the name to Lake George, after the King, which fact he made sure got back to London.

All this had taken time, for Johnson, who had got off to a late start anyway, was a slow mover.

It was at this time that Von Dieskau at Crown Point learned of Fort Edward, which had been barely begun, and determined to loop around Johnson's main body at the head of the lake and attack the small force building the fort. He made the move well enough, but at the last minute his Indians refused to attack. There was no use *commanding* Indians to do anything. They would simply disappear, hurt. So Von Dieskau sighed and turned north toward Lake

George. He had about 1,500 men, almost half of them Indians, and Johnson at the lake must have had twice that many, but Von Dieskau, entertaining a low opinion of colonials, did not hesitate.

Meanwhile, Johnson had heard of Von Dieskau's approach to Fort Edward, and he sent a force of about 1,000, under Colonel Ephraim Williams, to seek them out. "Old Hendricks" protested. "If to be killed, too many," he said. "If to fight, too few." But he was overruled.

A few miles south of the head of the lake this force was ambushed. The surprise was not complete, for certain overeager Indians on the French side gave it away, but it was effective enough to give the colonials a severe mauling.

"Old Hendricks" was killed. Colonel Williams was killed.[20] The Indians made no show of fighting but ran pell-mell back to the camp at the head of Lake George, where they spread the alarm. Many of the white men did the same, but a group of about 100 kept together and held the Frenchmen off, fighting an admirable retreat with all the aplomb of veterans.

When these heroes got back to camp they found that much had been done. Wagons had been grouped, trees felled, entrenchments dug; best of all, the cannons had been mounted and loaded with grape and canister.

Von Dieskau, despite the two-to-one odds, attacked. His Indians refused to go in, and his Canadians preferred to fight at a distance, but his regulars, true to tradition, fastened their bayonets and ran forward in close ranks, yelling. They were wonderful. They were cut down in swathes, but they would get up, yelling, and charge again—to be cut down again.[21]

This could not last. The Indians and Canadians, never coming out of cover, kept it up for a few hours; but there was not another charge. Some of the more hotheaded Americans, rasped by impatience, made a wild raid into the Indian-Canadian lines. Few had bayonets, and most had only camp hatchets, but they caused a near-panic, and, most unexpectedly, captured a general.

Von Dieskau, slightly wounded, was taken to the colonists' camp. He had not a word of English and, wishing to inform his captors who he was, he started to reach for his wallet in order to get his identification papers when a green guard, thinking that he was going for a pistol, shot him through both legs. Then, *really* wounded, he was taken to the tent of General Johnson, who himself had been nicked in one thigh by a musket ball.

The Indians, furious because of the death of "Old Hendricks," demanded that they be given General von Dieskau to replace him. They would have taken a long time killing Dieskau, of course; but Johnson, to his everlasting credit, refused, and sent the protégé of Marshal Saxe to England as a prisoner of war.

The French fell back, but they were not pursued. They ran spang into a force of colonial reinforcements coming up from the still uncompleted Fort Edward, and they were manhandled. They were badly disorganized by that time, only the regulars, or what was left of the regulars, keeping any kind of order. They could easily have been cut off from their boats, left in South Bay, Lake Champlain, in which case many of them would never get back to base. Lyman urged this course, as did others; but Johnson said that his men were tired and confused, and might get lost in such a movement.

The French did get back to Crown Point, and almost immediately they started to build another fort near there, at Ticonderoga, a fort much larger than Crown Point.

Johnson finished Fort Edward, but that was about all he did do. His men, short of supplies, were half mutinous. He never moved far from the head of Lake George, and in November he dismissed them—they would have left him anyway—and everybody went home.

The whole idea of the movement had been to capture

Crown Point, but Crown Point never had been even threatened, and the north-south invasion route still was firmly in the hands of the French.

Nevertheless, to the English at home the news coming so soon after the crushing report of Braddock's defeat looked at first like a glorious victory. A hero was needed. Lyman had conducted the latter part of the battle, including the action in which Von Dieskau had been captured, but Johnson made no mention of Lyman in his report. Also, Johnson had friends in London, friends in high places; and he had, after all, captured a real live lieutenant general in America, the first man ever to do this.

Parliament granted him £5,000 and made him a baronet—*Sir* William Johnson after this; while the dusky matron in the house on the banks of the Mohawk would thereafter be addressed as *Lady* Johnson.

7

A Latter-Day Diaspora

THE ONE BRIGHT SPOT in that woe-smitten summer of '55 was the capture of Fort Beauséjour, a feat that sealed the status of one of the most fought-over bits of real estate in the whole of the New World—that colorful peninsula that some called Acadia, some, Nova Scotia.

England and France had been enemies for centuries, and it was no more than natural that they should extend their enmity to America, where their first brush occurred in 1604 on this same trim peninsula. France claimed all the land north of the Spanish territories of Florida by reason of the voyages of exploration of Jacques Cartier and Giovanni da Verrazano; the English claimed the same territory by reason of the discoveries of the Cabots under Henry VII. The French were the first to plant a colony, a wobbly little place called Port Royal, in the land that they called Acadia, by which they meant virtually all the territory of what is now eastern Canada, roughly east of the Penobscot River—parts of Quebec and Maine, all of New Brunswick, and Cape Breton.

A few years later the English planted a colony and made it stick—for a while anyway—at Jamestown, Virginia. The governor of this colony in 1613, hearing vaguely of a French settlement to the north, sent a Captain Argall to seek out such a place and erase it. Argall found Port Royal and tore it down, either imprisoning its occupants or chasing them forth into the wilderness to live among the Micmacs, the Malecites, or the Abnakis, all Algonquins. That was eight years before the Pilgrims landed on or near Plymouth Rock.

There has been considerable question about the name Acadia. Some say that it was a Micmac word, Acadie or Acquoddy, meaning only "place" or "region," others that it derived from another Micmac word, Akade, meaning "camp" or "settlement." Still others profess to believe that Acadia is a corruption of Virgil's district of the Peloponnesus, Arcadia, home of pastoral simplicity, where everybody was happy all the time, especially the shepherds and shepherdesses. Sir Philip Sidney, too, was fascinated by this reputedly idyllic region.

But there was nothing in the least idyllic about Acadia, Canada, when it was first named. It was a land of swamps and harsh rocks, a land of terrible winters.

In no other part of Canada did England express any notable or lasting interest, but that one little peninsula, perhaps because of its privateering possibilities, its excellent harbors, seemed to fascinate her. As a consequence—for France never lost *her* interest—the place was pulled back and forth a great deal.

In 1621, James I graciously granted this land to one of his Scottish favorites, Sir William Alexander, who was soon to become the Earl of Sterling. The following year and the year after that, Sir William did try to populate it with Scots, who, however, dribbled back to their homeland, discouraged, while the few who remained mixed imperceptibly with the Indians and later with the French. It was Sir William who named the peninsula Nova Scotia, which is to say, of course, New Scotland.

Between 1633 and 1638 various feudal grantees, French noblemen, ignoring the English claim, brought over several hundreds of peasants, most of them from near La Rochelle. These were the original Acadians, the progenitors of those so famous in song and story. They were stubborn, quiet people. Though La Rochelle was noted as a den of Huguenots, the Acadians did not number any such among them, and were on the contrary devout Catholics. They obeyed unquestioningly the priests sent to them from Quebec.

They built dams and reclaimed land. It was not a place that blossomed like the rose at the slightest human touch. The Acadians had to work hard; but then, they had always worked hard. They took care of themselves, fed themselves, made their own clothes, and were never interested in building up trade with any other part of the world. They brought over from France vegetables and fruit trees and especially wheat, which did well under their patient care.

In 1654 one of Cromwell's admirals took over the peninsula by force, and the English held it for thirteen years after that, returning it to France at last by the Treaty of Breda when they had failed to get any of their own nationals to settle there.

Once again, in 1710, there being another war on at that time, it was by force that Great Britain got back Nova Scotia. When the war was finished and a treaty signed—the Treaty of Utrecht, April, 1713—it was stipulated that Cape Breton, Prince Edward Island, and all the other islands in the Gulf of St. Lawrence should be retained by France, but that Newfoundland and "all Nova Scotia or Acadia, with its ancient boundaries" should go to Great Britain forever. The name of Port Royal was changed to Annapolis in honor of the Queen. (Halifax was not founded until 1749, and was then named after the president of the Lords of Trade.)

There was a curious clause in the Treaty of Utrecht. It provided that any of the residents of Nova Scotia who wished to take the oath of allegiance to the British crown were to become British subjects. Any who refused were to seek homes elsewhere. They were given until the end of August, 1714, to make up their minds.

There were about 10,000 Acadians by this time, a sturdy, hard-headed lot. New France, always short of manpower, would gladly have taken them in and offered them land, especially on Prince Edward Island, which they called Isle St. Jean; but the Acadians, after looking over those lands, shook their heads. They did not elect to give up all they had worked so hard to develop, and they didn't think much of the rest of Canada. The British, they assumed, or hoped, were bluffing.

It seemed so. The deadline came and went, and nothing happened. Each side muttered excuses.

This went on for forty years. Again and again the home government insisted that the Acadians take an oath of allegiance to the throne, but the Acadians never did. Sometimes they squirmed out of it, and sometimes, trapped, they just hunkered down, shaking their heads, saying, "No."

Another war came, and the Acadians took no part in it. This was known in Europe as the War of the Austrian Succession, in most of the American colonies as King George's War, in New England, and not altogether playfully, as Governor Shirley's War. Its most important event, as far as Americans were concerned, was the taking of Fort Louisbourg on Cape Breton Island. The peninsula of Nova Scotia was not used as a main base in this monumental move, with which the Acadians had nothing to do; the colonists operated direct from various New England ports, especially Boston. Hundreds of Yankees died in that campaign, not so much from French lead as from disease, and hundreds of New England bodies were laid to rest in that bleak wintery shore.[22] However, France had taken Madras on the other side of the earth in that same multinominal war, and in the Treaty of

Aix-la-Chapelle, signed in April, 1748, the powers-that-be blithely swapped the one for the other, making New Englanders furious.

The Acadians stayed out of politics, minding their own business. They did not travel, they did not learn English, they were not taxed, they were allowed to practice their own religion, they were not called upon for military service, and they still refused to take that oath.

The situation was further complicated by the fact that while Great Britain believed that under the terms of the Treaty of Utrecht she was entitled not only to all the peninsula of Nova Scotia but also to most of New Brunswick and all the Gaspé peninsula, France contended that "Acadia" meant only the southern part of Nova Scotia. When war once again loomed, the French built a fort just north of the isthmus that attached Nova Scotia to the "mainland," territory that Great Britain claimed was her own. Britain responded by building and garrisoning Fort Lawrence exactly opposite the French place and only a few miles away.

Peace technically prevailed—the officers of the two forts often dined with one another and drank toasts together, which gave them a chance to spy—but nobody doubted that war was just over the horizon. What would happen then? There were about 350 British regulars stationed at Fort Lawrence, so near to Fort Beauséjour, and another 300 back at Annapolis; but there were some 12,000 Acadians. Could the commanding officer at Fort Lawrence afford to have *them* at his back when the chips were down and he faced Fort Beauséjour across the marshes? He did not think so.

The Acadians said that they did not care who won the not-yet war, but they were not convincing when they said this. Nobody doubted that all they wished to do was keep out of trouble, but fanatical priests could and did have their will with them, and they were threatened additionally by Indians friendly to the French. In British diplomatic correspondence they were designated the French Neutrals or the Neutral French, but just how neutral *were* they? How neutral *could* they be?

Governor Shirley of Massachusetts conferred with Governor Charles Lawrence of Nova Scotia, a bluff military man, a retired colonel, and they agreed that Fort Beauséjour must go. It would clear the isthmus, make the colony safer, and best of all shut the land route between Quebec and Louisbourg, since the governors were agreed that Louisbourg would have to be hit again as soon as there was war. Lawrence could spare only about 250 regulars, but Shirley, a dynamo, raised more than 2,000 New England militiamen, and they crossed the marshes, besieged Beauséjour, and took it, later to strengthen it and rename it Fort Cumberland. This was the only British success in that sad summer of '55, but it got very little attention in history, chiefly because of the story-book nature of what followed.

That hundreds of Acadians had helped in the original raising and later strengthening of Fort Beauséjour nobody questioned, though they themselves insisted that they had been forced. That they had "fingered" certain Indian raids was just as sure. Governor Lawrence, that old soldier, could only consider himself to be in the midst of the enemy, an intolerable situation. He did what he had to do, as he saw it.

He did not exile the Acadians on orders from King George II, as subsequent villain-seekers were to charge. The King was not even consulted. Nor did Lawrence act as directed by the Lords of Trade. He notified the Lords of his order, but he did not ask their permission.

He did consult with his council and with the two admirals who were in Nova Scotia at the time, and he did depend upon Shirley's New Englanders to do the dirty work, but the decision was his own, and it was purely a military one.

He rounded up as many of the Acadians as he could—about half of them, or 6,000. The others escaped either to the Canadian "mainland" or to one of the Gulf islands, or to Miquelon or St. Pierre, or they slipped back into the forest to mingle with the Indians. Their houses were burned, lest these serve as an inducement to return.

Those who escaped to Canada were horribly exploited by the corrupt officials of New France, and they died like flies. Those who remained were unceremoniously dumped upon the Atlantic seaboard colonies, where they were not wanted.

Every attempt was made to see that families were not broken up, but this sometimes did happen. Large supplies of food had been stocked, but what with one delay and another it was late fall before the final shipload of exiles got off, and inevitably there was some suffering.

What was extraordinary about the business was not Lawrence's decision, which could be defended or disputed, but the fact that he seems to have made no preliminary arrangements. Perhaps this was because he feared that a master plan would mean that the secret of the project would leak out? In any event, instead of warning the various governors of the Atlantic colonies, or even asking their permission, he simply dumped exiles ashore here and there, seemingly without any schedule or blueprint.

Georgia flatly refused to accept its unwanted allotment. It would not even let them land, and it was up to the skippers of the various vessels that carried them to find them some other home.

It might have been supposed that South Carolina, and especially Charleston, with its large French population, would welcome these refugees. But the Charleston French were Huguenots, and the Acadians were Papists, and religious hatred dies hard. The kicked-outs met no sympathy in South Carolina.

Pennsylvania was kinder, Massachusetts and Connecticut kindest of all.

Henry Callister in Maryland, Anthony Benezet in Penn-

EMBARKING THE YOUNG ACADIANS

sylvania, and Thomas Hutchinson in Massachusetts were notably gentle—and efficient. They devoted themselves to the thankless task of making these uninvited visitors, if not comfortable, at least fed.

Too often the Acadians—a dirty lot, suggestive of Gypsies, unwilling to work, refusing even to try to learn the language—camped at the edges of cities; but Connecticut and Massachusetts spread them under prepared plans, treating them in small batches like the public poor. In Connecticut, for instance, they were distributed according to the sizes of the towns to take them: Norwich and New Haven 19 each, Fairfield 17, Middletown 16, Farmington and Stratford 14 each, Hartford 13, Ashford, Haddam, Bolton, and Enfield three each.

Some, not many, settled in the cities where they found themselves, setting up unassimilable little colonies of their own: the South Charles Street section of Baltimore, for instance, is still sometimes called French Town.

Some, ill-advised by their own sea lawyers,[23] roundly declared that they were prisoners of war and therefore could not be made to work; they insisted that they be fed while idle. This did not ingratiate them to their hosts.

The business was badly botched. Some of the Acadians did not hesitate to complain about the accommodations. Most of them kept talking about going back, and in a few cases they were given money to do so—money they accepted without shame, for they had fallen to feeling very sorry for themselves. A few found their way to Martinique in the West Indies, where at least they were among French people. Others, rather more, got to New Orleans, a sympathetic city; and their descendants still live in that neighborhood, the name "Cajun" being a corruption of "Acadian." A large number eventually returned to Nova Scotia, where they did in fact become British subjects, if not very enthusiastic ones; but the war had been over for a long while by then.

8

The Irreconcilables

It was May 18, 1756, two years almost to the day after George Washington had started the shooting, when Great Britain, at last, almost absent-mindedly, got around to declaring war on France, which retaliated.

These formalities made no difference in the upper-level thinking in both nations, which had been going on at a furious pace all the long winter.

In France the decision already had been made to send to Canada a real military man, a full-time professional, rather than to clothe the governor-general in military garb from time to time. The trouble was, the two posts were not clearly differentiated, and for the rest of the history of New France there was always to be a strain between the governor-general and the commanding general. Where did the power of one start, that of the other end? It could lead to confusion, though this was not immediately evident far away in France.

The man the ministers picked for the supreme military post was Lieutenant General Louis Joseph Montcalm de Saint Veran, Marquis de Montcalm, a short, dapper man in his middle forties, a man for whom the word "gallant" might have been coined. At that age—and he was a devoted family man—he might have thought that he was entitled to rest; but he didn't complain; he strapped on his sword and went to work, and they sent some good soldiers along with him.

Meanwhile, the ministers of Great Britain, not one of whom was an intellectual giant, had been discussing at a series of conferences the choice of a successor to Major General Shirley.

At Braddock's death Shirley, the ranking major general in America, had automatically become commander in chief of all His Majesty's forces there. But Shirley was not the man for that job, as even the ministers knew. Astute politician though he was, efficient, fast, energetic, he had had no conventional military experience and in the course of his long governorship he had made many enemies in America, men who could scarcely be expected to rally around him as he and the other governors had rallied more or less around General Braddock. That would be the commander in chief's first duty—to bring the Atlantic colonies together, to get them to work in harness.

The ministers considered Lord Tyrawley, Sir John Mordaunt, Lieutenant General Cholmondeley, Lord George Sackville, and they also considered Lord Panmure, Lord Howe, Colonel Conway, Colonel Cornwallis, and Colonel Abercromby. They settled at last upon John Campbell, 4th Earl of Loudoun.

Loudoun was a Scot, but by no means dour. He was a short man and thickset, rich, with a high complexion and a jolly twinkling eye. He and Montcalm would have liked one another. They never did meet.

Loudoun traveled in style, his baggage and his private stock of wine taking up virtually all the hold space in one transport, while he was personally attended by no fewer than seventeen civilian body servants, including one of his mistresses, whose name was Jean Masson. He had also three coaches and nineteen horses.

He had been led to believe that he would be given 17,000 men. In fact he got somewhat fewer than half of that number, still a much larger body than Braddock had commanded. Many of the regular regiments, however, had to be "fleshed out" to full strength, ten companies of 70 men each, by colonial enlistments. The 44th, the 47th, 48th, 50th, and 51st, for instance, eventually were two-thirds to three-fourths American. This was a practice that Lord Loudoun, a soldier's soldier if ever there was one, deplored; but he had no choice.

Loudoun made New York his headquarters, but he got around a good deal. His powers were wide.[24] For all his conviviality he was a prodigious worker. He always had a mountain of paper work, and his biggest task remained that of getting the colonies to pull together. Much of his work was done directly with the various governors, and here he was lucky, for just at that time the governors of the British colonies in America were a superior lot, as colonial governors went—Shirley of Massachusetts, Hopkins of Rhode Island, Wentworth of New Hampshire, Fitch of Connecticut, Hardy and DeLancey of New York, Sharpe of Maryland, Dinwiddie of Virginia, Dobbs and Lyttleton of the Carolinas.

The only one of these with whom Loudoun did not get along was Shirley. Here he was not alone. The ablest of the governors, Shirley was also the least liked. It was not just because he gave himself airs; it was rather that, an outspoken man, he had no patience with bungling. He was shrewd and farsighted, but his cavalier shortcuts in military matters gave Lord Loudoun inexpressible pain.

Loudoun did not have to endure him long. Shirley, who at first had got along well enough with his fellow amateur major general, William Johnson, had fallen to feuding with this personage, who still had his friends in court. Shirley had spats, too, with the other governors, who worked with Johnson against him, so that soon he found himself recalled not exactly in disgrace but not in very good odor either. There is no reason to believe that Loudoun had any part in this cabal, but he undoubtedly approved of its results, especially since Shirley's successor, Thomas Pownall, was a man after his own heart.

Loudoun could manipulate the bickering colonies just as much as these governors could manipulate their respective assemblies, which was very little. The assemblies refused to vote the supplies requested. They declared embargoes against one another. They scorned one another's currency. They were hard to deal with.

His lordship's assignment called not only for military knowledge and a liberal dash of diplomacy but also for a knowledge of banking. He had to handle pistoles, half-johannes, gold moidores, Spanish and Portuguese eight-real pieces, German carolines, French guineas, and light and heavy doubloons. The value of these coins was different in the different colonies, and was changing all the time. Also, Shirley's carelessness with accounts confused the meticulous Scot.

Moreover, the man did not have a real, whole army to begin with. To all intents and purposes, what with the colonial inserts, he had to create his own army and to train it anew. He was intelligent enough to see that European methods were not enough in America, and he insisted that his infantrymen be taught to fire and to load in a prone position, also that the members of flanking parties when attacked should take shelter behind trees. Such tactics shocked the regulars, who had always been told that exposure was a requisite and that to take cover was to display cowardice and might bring about a panic. But Loudoun persisted.

Lord Loudoun did not originate the Rangers idea, but he did give this movement his blessing, without which it would surely have died. Just before the arrival of Lord Loudoun, Robert Rogers, a burly country man of dubious antecedents, had proposed to Governor Shirley the enlistment of a company of sixty Rangers, with himself as captain; and Shirley had agreed and had issued a commission. The problem was an old one with the English: the difficulty of getting Indians, even unreliable ones, to act as scouts. What Rogers proposed was a force of white bushfighters. But he and his followers did not propose to do the work for beads. They demanded pay, higher pay indeed than the British regulars got, and to this, too, Governor Shirley had assented.

The Rangers have proved to be more popular with subsequent romancers than they ever were with their fellow members of His Majesty's armed forces in America. They were a dirty, hard-drinking lot who had scant respect for any sort of discipline. When they were engaged upon the work for which they had been hired they were incomparable, but when there was nothing for them to do they were bad for morale. That extra pay rankled; and then, too, the Rangers were not required to do ordinary camp chores—to stand guard, to maintain latrines and the rest—which fact did not endear them to the regulars.

Nevertheless, Loudoun thought that the Rangers made up the answer to a vexing question, and he not only tolerated them but also caused them to increase in number, company by company, while Rogers himself was promoted to major.

There was even one Ranger company consisting of "tame" Indians, fifty Stockbridges, with their own officers, Captain Jacob Cheeksaunkun, Lieutenant Jacob Naunaughtaunk, and Ensign Solomon Uhauavamut; but these never did amount to much.

Without ever losing the twinkle in his eye, then, the 4th Earl of Loudoun succeeded in getting a great deal of work done in the American colonies that summer and autumn. However, it was not work that his friends could boast about at home. It was work that did not *show*. It involved no clash of arms; and indeed there was nothing about it that would indicate that Lord Loudoun was winning the war—or was even *fighting* the war.

This seeming sloth was pointed up by the whirlwind of activities indulged in by milord's opposite number to the north.

The Marquis de Montcalm had his political troubles too. The governor-general of Canada, Pierre François de Rigaud, Marquis de Vaudreuil-Cavagnal, a Canadian born, and an older man, was intensely jealous of him, not infrequently overriding his decisions, and all the while trying to cut the ground from under his feet by means of letters to friends at home. Montcalm to a considerable extent offset this by staying in the field.

Just at first it was difficult for the Indians to take him seriously, he was so short. But they soon learned.

He first visited Crown Point, and shook his head. He stimulated the erection of the much larger and stronger fort nearby on Ticonderoga Point, a structure the French called Fort Carillon. This was a stone star-shaped building in the approved Vauban style, with ditch, covered way, all sorts of outworks. Montcalm strove to make it as nearly impregnable as could be, for he saw instantly the importance of controlling Lake Champlain, something that the British were slow to perceive.

After that the energetic little man set out in full force, by way of the St. Lawrence, for Oswego. He had no trouble taking this poorly prepared place after what could be thought no more than a token defense, thereby rendering the still unfinished British war vessels in Lake Ontario useless. With one stroke, using some of the guns that had been taken from Braddock, Montcalm had sealed the western frontier. The nearest English soldier was more than 160 miles away.

The capture of Fort Oswego was hailed by the French as a very great victory, as indeed it was in its consequences. It was hardly *glorious*, however, for it was marred by the behavior of the Indian allies who, after the surrender, smashed into the hospital and scalped all the sick and wounded. How

many of these there had been was never clearly established—
the French were reticent about releasing such figures—but
it was a nasty business, no matter what the count.

News of the loss of Oswego hit London a stunning blow.
Everybody wondered why nobody seemed to have seen the
importance of the place in time.

The war on the continent of Europe also was going
badly for Great Britain, with her captain-general the Duke
of Cumberland proving himself to be somewhat less than a
shrewd strategist, especially when contrasted with Frederick
of Prussia, Frederick the Great, who, with Britain behind
him, financing him, was battling most of the rest of Europe.[25]
Cumberland fell from favor, even with his own father the
King. He resigned all his commissions and offices and retired
to private life, from which he was never to return.

This move would have been made inevitable anyway,
after the meteoric rise to power, in early December, of a man
who believed that war was too serious a business to be left
to the generals, just as politics was too serious to be left to
politicians. Only William Pitt, William Pitt averred, could
manage these momentous matters.

9

Up Above the World So High

"H<small>E</small> [<small>THE EMPEROR OF</small> L<small>ILLIPUT</small>] is taller by almost the breadth of my nail than any of his court, which alone is enough to strike an awe into the beholders," Dean Swift had written a little earlier. So it was with William Pitt. Here was not an age of greatness; and had he not been surrounded by minnows he never would have looked like a whale.

Pitt was not the most powerful man in the kingdom, though he was the most admired. Everything about him was stupendous, splendid; everything glittered; it was inconceivable that he ever had been a boy, much less a baby. He had fine flashing eyes, an accipitrine nose, a majestic manner, and when he addressed the House of Commons the members, silent, O-mouthed, listened. The members loved to hear him make a speech. But though they applauded, they would not vote for him afterward. Dutiful fellows, they voted as they had been bribed.

Presiding over the pie counter was that high-strung wretch the Duke of Newcastle, a Pelham. His was a refined system, made smooth by age. The bribes were mostly in the form of appointments, sinecures, though there was some cash.

The imperious Pitt had nothing to do with this corruption. He was above that, as he was above virtually everything, for he lived in the clouds. He said it so often and so eloquently that men were beginning to believe that he was in truth the only man who could win the war, yet how could he become first minister if he did not know how to operate the machine?

There was another difficulty. The King couldn't stand the sight of him.

Unexpectedly, the public liked him. He was hailed as the Great Commoner, though he was quick enough to accept a title when it was offered. His forensic triumphs in the Commons were only hearsay, for they were never published, and he did not deign to address the mob out of doors, yet he was popular with the people, whose voice, while not loud, was insistent. Members of Parliament as well came to believe that perhaps William Pitt was, after all, the only person who could win this long and hideously expensive war.

He was made secretary of state and leader of the House. And the Duke of Newcastle, though he still had the votes of a large majority of both houses in his pocket, was out. Mr. Pitt had made it clear that he would not consent to serve in any cabinet that included his grace of Newcastle.

This was an anomalous state of affairs, and it could not last. In April, before he had succeeded in bringing about many of the sweeping reforms he planned, Pitt was out. But Newcastle was not back in.

For eleven weeks Great Britain had no government at all. It bumbled along somehow, but the war suffered.

A compromise was called for. Pitt unbent long enough to agree to one. He would be back in power again, more firmly than ever, but Newcastle would be a member of his cabinet. What it amounted to was that Pitt should take care of the oratory and the war while Newcastle took care of the patronage. No longer obliged to act like a politician, the Commoner could spend all his time being a statesman.

Even before he could have been sure of himself in the saddle, and well before the spring-summer vacation he was perforce given, Pitt had taken over the direction of the war in America. Without any warning or apology he had started to correspond directly with the colonial governors, urging them to cooperate in the effort to beat the French. In other words, from 3,000 miles away he was directing men he didn't know to move about in a country he had not visited, and to do thus-and-so like that many performing dogs at the sound of their master's whip-crack, and all this without any preliminary consultation with the specialist who had been assigned to the task in the first place.

If Lord Loudoun found this disconcerting, as he must have done, he made no complaint—publicly. The Commoner at least would keep the supplies coming, and the reinforcements, for he spent money like water and was known to believe that the war in America, so far from being a sideshow, was a contest that would change the whole course of history.

It had been Loudoun's plan greatly to strengthen and to fortify the northern route to Quebec, the Lake George–Lake Champlain–Richelieu River route, concentrating his forces there. Mr. Pitt vetoed this plan. The Lake Champlain country, he decreed, should be lightly guarded, while the main effort should be against Fort Louisbourg. Loudoun had no choice but to acquiesce, though it was against his better judgment.

Northern New York, then, was left in charge of a brigadier, a hypochondriac named Webb, who was more interested in the state of his palsy than in the condition and distribution of his men, all militia. Webb arrived late on the scene from New York City and spent most of his time at William Johnson's Fort Edward near the great curve of the Hudson, rather than at Fort William Henry at the southern end of Lake George.

William Henry, an irregular square with four bastions,

built of timber cribbing filled with earth and gravel and faced with logs, was the farthest north of any English post, the natural base for an invasion of Canada, and as such understandably a place of concern to the enemy. The previous summer a British army engineer had examined it and made sundry suggestions for its strengthening—suggestions that had not been acted upon. Late in February of the new year 1757, a band of 1,600 Frenchmen and Indians, traveling on snowshoes, had tried a surprise attack upon Fort William Henry. They had no fieldpieces, and when the surprise failed their raid was doomed. Major William Eyre and the garrison of 350 easily held them off. The invaders did burn some boats, but soon they had to retreat to Canada lest they starve, and that was the end of that.

The raid, a brilliant one, for all its failure, had been the brain child of the governor-general, who acted without consultation with the Marquis de Montcalm, putting his own brother in charge. When summer came, and with it Montcalm's turn, the matter was more conventionally done. Montcalm knew that Loudoun's regulars and many of his militiamen were in Nova Scotia, preparing for a stroke against Fort Louisbourg, and he meant to take advantage of this fact. When early in August he left Quebec it was with about 1,800 Indians and 6,000 white soldiers, about half of them militia. Of the Indians, fewer than half were "Christianized," which is to say at least a little civilized, but the rest were wild tribesmen from the west, who practiced cannibalism.

The fort had been reinforced, and Lieutenant Colonel Monro had about 2,000 men. Still, he sent to General Webb for further reinforcements, which Webb promised. The general, however, did not leave Fort Edward.

Montcalm drew his lines and brought up his artillery. He had some big guns, and it became clear from the beginning that unless there was a considerable relief the siege would be a success. Monro wrote again for reinforcements, and this time Webb answered him by saying that he could not spare any troops and suggesting that Monro surrender while he could still get good terms. The siege at that time had lasted only six days.

The second message from Webb fell into the hands of the French, and Montcalm must have smiled as he read the translation. The original he caused to be sent on to Colonel Monro, under a flag of truce.

Monro's own officers in council assembled already had advised him to ask for terms, and this he did. They were unexpectedly easy, those terms. The English colonials could keep their muskets, though they must give up their powder and all their other supplies. The French promised to protect them from any manhandling on the part of the redskins, and would tell off a guard of 400 soldiers to escort them to Fort Edward.

The truth is, Montcalm would have granted almost any terms, for his men were starving and he knew that the English colonists had stored in Fort William Henry enough food rations for 6,000 men for six weeks. He had dug his trenches and mounted his guns in a cool, deliberate manner, as though he had all the time in the world; but he was gambling on an early capitulation, and Webb's second message must have been a godsend.

The evacuation was a disorderly business, and bloody. Somehow the Indians had got to the rum, and many of them were violently drunk. They scalped the inmates of the sick bay. They pushed, tripped, cuffed, and tore the clothes off the retiring New England and New York militiamen, leaving some of them nearly naked, and they stole everything they could get their hands on. Then they went utterly berserk and started to lay about them with their tomahawks, all the while screaming at the top of their lungs. Scalping knives flashed.

The Canadians did nothing about it, nor did the French soldiers. The French officers, to give them credit, did all that they could, many of them risking their own lives.

The few women and children who were there were of

course killed and scalped. They were among the first to go.

The estimates of those massacred range from 60 to 150. Nobody will ever know for sure. Large numbers, at least upwards of 400, were made prisoners, and these could expect a much slower death than had been meted out to their companions, but the French, properly ashamed of themselves, "bought back" most of these, paying brandy and gunpowder for them, and saw that they were escorted to the road home. They didn't get all. One prisoner the wild western Indians boiled in the public square in Montreal the night they got back, and they ate him there, making a big to-do about it.

Meanwhile Loudoun was having his difficulties with the Louisbourg expedition. After the first harsh orders from Mr. Pitt and after the initial shock of learning that the Great Commoner was communicating directly with the colonial governors, laying the law down to them, Lord Loudoun felt an easing of the commands, his friends in London having got to work for him. Then there was the hiatus, the eleven weeks when there was no government, and, though Pitt came back into power late in July, it was almost September before his renewed orders could reach the man in America.

Loudoun, first-off, was left in doubt as to how many men he should leave in New York under Webb, because he did not know the nature of the regiments he would receive. Pitt had promised him guns, and *being* Pitt he could be counted upon to deliver these, but Loudoun did not know their sizes or whether they were of iron or of brass, important considerations in his planning. He did not know whether to expect Navy vessels in New York or whether he must go to Halifax for them, and when at last he did sail for Halifax it was with a dangerously small escort.

He made connection with the Navy, but already the summer was far advanced. Ordinarily the island of Cape Breton, where bleak Fort Louisbourg was located, was shrouded in fog late in the spring and early in the summer, but this year the fog seldom left and never for more than a few hours at a time. Moreover, the French Navy had got there first. Eight French warships were waiting in the Louisbourg harbor, and the British naval force could not be expected to tackle them except under ideal conditions. Time after time their scout vessels came back with the same report: it simply wasn't safe, the weather being what it was.

Loudoun strove to keep his men busy digging trenches and playing war games, which old-timers thought rather silly. He also raised a large number of cabbages and other vegetables there at Halifax that summer. He was to be much criticized for this, but he never did assign more than twenty soldiers to gardening duty at a time, and, in a place where fresh vegetables were unobtainable since the Acadians had been driven away, he wanted to guard against an outbreak of scurvy.

At last they held a council of war. Such councils were not popular at the time, it being thought that they were only devices to evade the responsibility of an unfortunate decision. The members of the one at Halifax—four major generals, including the earl himself, and the two highest ranking naval officers—were well aware of this feeling. They sat for nine days, heard twenty witnesses, and recorded every word of it. They decided at last that the expedition should be withdrawn for that season.

As if to confirm this decision there rose a hurricane, the worst blow anybody there ever had known, and the ships in the bay were scattered. One was sunk, twelve were dismasted, all naval vessels. That settled it. They went back to New York and New England.

Only a few months before, in March, a well-connected admiral, Byng, had been shot by order of a court-martial because in a scrape in the Mediterranean he had failed "to do his Utmost." It could happen again, and to a general. They knew this, and Lord Loudoun, especially, knew it. All the same, they called the expedition off.

Pitt was furious. Loudoun was recalled.

10

A Soldier of the King

Lord Jeffery Amherst was a soldier of the King,
And he came from across the sea.
To the Frenchmen and the Indians he didn't do a thing
In the wilds of this wild countree.[26]

DIVISION IS A MILITARY SIN, concentration of forces a
virtue. Mr. Pitt must have felt supremely strong when he
arranged for the campaign of '58 to consist of three different
expeditions striking in three separate directions.

The officer who was to lead in person the easternmost
action, the siege of Louisbourg, was Jeffery Amherst, jumped
from a colonelcy to a major generalship for the occasion. He
had been handpicked by Pitt, and it was a curious choice.
Amherst was in his early forties and a capable soldier with
a solid if not bright record, but though he came of a good
family he was not aristocratic, not distinguished, not rich,
and had no political connections. He was a plodder, but
neat. He would leave no loose ends. It might have been
thought that *speed* was what the impatient Pitt most wanted,
and if so he would never get it from Jeffery Amherst.

GENERAL JAMES WOLFE

There were three brigadiers on Amherst's staff. Two of these showed no departure from tradition, but the third, a lad just turned thirty-one, is memorable.

James Wolfe came of a military family, and the army was in his heart. He was a tall, gangling man, awkward, hatchet-faced, with a receding chin. Sometimes he wore a wig, and when he did it was likely to be slightly askew; and at other times he wore his own hair, which was red. He was highly emotional and given to reciting poetry, especially Gray's "Elegy Written in a Country Churchyard," his favorite. He was intense, passionate, and had no sense of humor. Even as an army officer he was unorthodox: for instance, he disapproved of flogging, a practice that the old-timers were sure was the only thing that held the army together. When he didn't like a man or a thing—and there were many such— he said so, emphatically.

There were four companies of Rangers at the siege of Louisbourg, and they were out of place in that formal type of warfare, waged on a barren rock, so they showed at their worst. *"Canaille,"* James Wolfe called them.[27] Moreover, Wolfe went on to express the same opinion of all Americans, though idle Rangers were the only ones he had seen. "The Americans are in general the dirtiest, most contemptible cowardly dogs that you can conceive," he wrote to Lord George Sackville. "There is no depending on them in action." [28]

Wolfe did not boast. He did not need to. His regiment was one of the best in the service, perhaps *the* best. He never spared himself. Many men disliked him, but nobody who knew him failed to respect him.

Wolfe had charge of the landing near Louisbourg on June 4. There were 157 warships and transports drawn up just outside the bay, and inside there were 5 French ships of the line and 7 frigates, with a total of 544 guns and about 3,000 sailors, who, however, owing largely to interservice rivalry, were to take precious little part in the fighting. Inside the fort and manning the many outworks were six battalions of regulars, two battalions of foreign volunteers, twenty-four companies of militia, and two companies of regular artillerymen, somewhat more than 3,000 all told. In addition there were about 4,000 civilians, for Louisbourg was more than just a big fort: it was a major fishing center and privateers' hangout.

For two days the vessels from Nova Scotia could not even venture close to shore, but then the fog disappeared, the wind that swept it away kicking up breakers that streamed toward the rocky shore. It was a touch-and-go operation. Almost by accident one small group found an unguarded

GENERAL WOLFE BRINGING HIS MEN ASHORE AT LOUISBOURG

stretch of coast and piled in. Wolfe, who had been about to give the signal for retreat, took prompt advantage of this opening, and soon he had all his men ashore.

Getting the guns on land was a harder matter, and then platforms had to be built for them, and roads built to get them within range of the fort. It was a backbreaking, heartbreaking business.

Louisbourg was no wilderness shack. Made largely of sea sand and the porphyritic trap-rock from a nearby quarry, it had thick walls, thick bastions, all manner of well-placed outworks. It had taken the wild New Englanders of thirteen years before exactly seven days to smash it, but the newcomers would be lucky if they did the job in that many weeks, for Louisbourg in the meanwhile had been enormously strengthened, especially since the previous summer, when Loudoun had come so close to attacking it.

Once the big guns were ashore and set up there was no question of the result. It was only a matter of time. The siege was a typical European operation, the first in America.[29] Lines of circumvallation were drawn and trenches, approaches, and gun pits dug. Closer and closer the British drew, on all sides, laboriously bringing up their big weapons, monotonously pounding the fort to rubble. It might take all summer, but they would do it. They had assembled prefabricated blockhouses at strategic spots, and they were there to stay.

All this while Major General James Abercromby was assembling his host in the Hudson River valley for the purpose of forcing the Champlain-Richelieu route. Abbie-Pamby the men called him, Abbie, short for Abigail, being the name then current for a fussy old woman. William Pitt has been praised by later generations for picking young men to command, the implication being that until his time the fuddy-duddies had ruled the British Army, though the only young Pitt appointee ever named is Wolfe. Certainly Amherst was

MAJOR GENERAL JAMES ABERCROMBY

no dashing figure; his experience and his ideas were similar
to those of Braddock, though Amherst was more lucky. As
for Abercromby, at the time he was put in charge of the
largest conventional army ever assembled in America he was
fifty-two, which by prevalent reckoning meant that he was
tottering on the edge of the grave. He was a Scot, and exceedingly cautious. Walpole called him "a commander whom
a child might outwit, or terrify with a popgun." [30]

The best thing about Abercromby was his second-in-
command, George Augustus, Viscount Howe, colonel of the
crack 55th and with the "in America" rank of brigadier
general. Lord Howe was thirty-four. He did not find the

provincials distasteful, boorish; rather, he liked them, and gladly mingled with them. Though his background was Germanic—indeed it was said that he was a cousin of the King on the left-hand side—he had no fondness for the pipe-clayed, spit-and-polish methods so popular on the continent of Europe and so much in favor with the Duke of Cumberland when he was captain-general of the British Army.

Howe had it as his motto: When in America, fight as the Americans do. He took Robert Rogers, still a mere captain, as his model—and his instructor. He cast aside his finery, donned a hunter's shirt, and followed the rough ones into the woods. He learned about bush-loping the hard way. He was an irregular of irregulars; and when his course of instruction had ended he started to teach the members of his own regiment what he had learned. He cut off their coat tails, he wrapped their lower legs in canvas gaiters, he commanded them to carry an emergency ration of corn meal so that they could be independent in the wilderness for days and even weeks on end. His officers, deprived of their washerwomen and even of their batmen, and forbidden to take pomatum and champagne into the field, had no enthusiasm for this new austerity; but, though Lord Howe was a strict disciplinarian, his men adored him.[31]

There was something else, besides its size, that marked this army apart from any other ever assembled in America: it was the first to be issued rifles.

Since the passing of the pike the musket had been the standard infantry weapon, a short hand-cannon that went off with a tremendous bang, propelling a ball perhaps 100 yards, sometimes even a little farther, though with no degree of accuracy. The musket, being smooth-bored, was easy to reload. The rifle was something else again. Men, especially sportsmen, had been using rifles for many years. No one person can be credited with the invention of this gun. Lately the German mercenaries, the Hessians and Hanoverians in particular, had been issuing rifles to members of a special scouting corps called Jaegers, men who were mostly ex-woodsmen, ex-gamekeepers. These weapons, however, were short and heavy, not at all like the so-called Kentucky rifle, which was also made by Germans, emigrants, not in Kentucky but in western Pennsylvania.

Soldiers were wary of the rifle. It would shoot farther and with much more accuracy than the Brown Bess, the British Army's standard musket, but its great length made it hard to reload from a kneeling position, impossible from a prone position, and just because it *was* rifled it gave the ramrod a fight all the way down. A good musketeer could easily get in two shots while a rifle man was reloading his piece, and that second shot might mean his life.

The rifles issued to Abercromby's men had been manufactured in England on the model of the western Pennsylvania rifle. Only ten were allotted to each regiment of regulars, none at all to the militia. The thing obviously was regarded as an experiment, and since nothing more was to be heard of it for many years it must be considered an experiment that failed. Not until well after the War of 1812 did the rifle really begin to come into its own as a military weapon. The Revolution was fought almost entirely with muskets, on both sides. The rifle then was looked upon as a freak of the wild frontier.

Abercromby was commander in chief of all the King's military forces in America, though he could not give orders to Amherst besieging Louisbourg. He had served under Lord Loudoun, and he surely must have known about the difficulties of raising provincial troops, who were always late. The plan called for a start north from Fort Edward early in May, so that Fort Carillon (Ticonderoga) could be caught with only its winter garrison, but it was the end of June before all the militia was in and ready to march. July 4 the real start was made, in 800 bateaux and 90 whaleboats, from the southern end of Lake George. July 7 the bulk of the force, numbering some 15,000, the largest army in the history of North America,[32] landed at the upper end of the channel that joins Lake George with Lake Champlain. That channel, only a few miles long, was not navigable because of rapids. The French had built a bridge over it, but they had destroyed this only the previous day, and a vanguard of about 350 Frenchmen was waiting to dispute the landing.

The brushing-off of this harassment was scarcely more than the work of minutes, and the Frenchmen, their ranks intact, faded back into the wilderness. It was assumed that they would return to the fort a few miles away, and that's what they had meant to do, but they seemed to have brought no Indian guides and they got lost in the wilderness and began to flounder around here and there.

A force consisting largely of Rangers, and headed by Lord Howe in person, pushed into that wilderness in the direction of Ticonderoga, their purpose being to reconnoiter the fort and also to make sure that the vanguard had truly retreated there. And *they* got lost.

The two parties stumbled into one another, each astounded. There was a brisk exchange of shots, and the French broke and ran. The English did not pursue. They had lost only a few men dead in that shoot-out, but one of these was George Augustus, Viscount Howe. He lay there in buckskin, a general officer who thought that his place was in the front line with the men.[33]

Abercromby did not know what to do, so he did nothing. He just camped where he found himself at the foot of Lake George, until the next day.

The Marquis de Montcalm had been busy. He had fewer than 4,000 troops in Fort Carillon, which, though it had been enlarged, could not hold all of them, so that many were stationed in a nearby fortified camp. Carillon sat on a rocky promontory that thrust itself out into Lake Champlain in

THE WHALEBOAT EXPEDITION AGAINST TICONDEROGA

the direction of Vermont. They were good troops, the French, but their leader did not think that he ought to pit them man-for-man against the English army, which was almost four times as large, so he set them to work chopping down trees, officers and men alike.

They cleared away all the timber on a ridge half a mile west of the fort proper, built a breakwork topped with sandbags and cut with loopholes, and from the severed branches and upper trunks assembled an abatis—that is, a barrier of branches sticking out toward an expected enemy, their ends spiked. He did this all in one day.

The ridge was only about a quarter of a mile across, and it sloped down sharply to the water on either side, making it a strong position.

Abercromby could have looped around to the north of Fort Carillon, easily taking the decrepit Crown Point, and cutting Montcalm off from supplies or reinforcements. He could have placed a battery on the top of Mount Defiance, whence he could bombard the very middle of Fort Carillon, the guns of which could not be elevated enough to answer this bombardment. Or he might have brought up his heaviest guns and hammered the abatis to pieces, afterward hammering the fort itself likewise.

He had plenty of weapons. He had four 18-pounders, six 12-pounders, eight brass royals, and any number of mortars, one of them an enormous 13-incher. He had the ammunition too: many tons of powder, and 200 balls for each cannon.

He did not use these. He had got it into his head somehow that there were 6,000 men in Fort Carillon and that another 3,000 were on their way from Canada. Any of the conventional attacks would have taken a little time, though it would have been comparatively bloodless; but Abercromby did not think that he could spare the time. He sent out a couple of engineers, who obviously did not know their business, and they scouted a bit, to report back that a frontal attack was perfectly feasible. So Abercromby ordered a frontal attack, with bayonets.

Of all the courses open to him this was the worst.

The result was disaster. Rank after rank, the British were mowed down by men they could not even see, much less reach. When at last they fell back, and General Abercromby was notified (he stayed in a sawmill two miles away throughout the action) he could think of nothing but to order another frontal attack. And once again the men went in, and once again were slaughtered. By this time the sharpened branches of the abatis were fairly festooned with the dead and dying. Abercromby ordered another frontal attack.

This went on for more than five hours. Once a few of the Highlanders actually did get to and over that log breastwork, and they laid about them for a little while with their claymores until they were cut down. Nobody ever did get anywhere near the fort itself.

The French lost fewer than 350. The British loss was close to 2,000, including more than 1,600 regulars, the best in the army. The 42nd Highland Regiment alone (the Black Watch) lost 499 men, more than half of their number.

The retreat was worse than that; it was a rout. The French made no move to pursue, for they never supposed that the British were falling back for any other reason than to reform. Instead, the men who had fought magnificently all afternoon were seized by panic. They were safe now, but they did not seem to know it. They dropped everything, even their muskets, and ran for the boats. All the cannons were left behind, all the ammunition, all the supplies. They did not stop until they had reached their old camp at the far end of Lake George, and one of the first to arrive there was Major General James Abercromby. He frittered away the rest of the summer, doing nothing, and when, in October,

General Amherst was free to join him, they agreed that it was too late to make any decisive movement that season and they went into winter quarters.

For the siege of Louisbourg was ended. The British Army and the Royal Navy had cooperated perfectly, and the Gibraltar of America had capitulated on July 26 after a long, determined defense. There were honors for both sides.

Orders had been to go up the St. Lawrence and besiege Quebec if time and conditions allowed, but Amherst and his brigadiers agreed that Quebec would have to wait for another year. Wolfe was assigned the unpleasant task of sacking and burning every little fishing village and even individual huts along the edges of the Gulf of St. Lawrence, in order to weaken the city up the river, a task he accomplished with his usual thoroughness, while Jeffery Amherst went to New York to report in person to his superior officer.

The news of the fall of Louisbourg, coming as it did so soon after the shaking news of Abercromby's defeat, was received with joy throughout the English-speaking world, and especially in New England, where God was thanked with a vehemence virtually unprecedented. The Yankee always had feared Louisbourg as a fitting-out place for privateers.

There were other assuagements. For one, there was Captain John Bradstreet, the boat specialist. Bradstreet was an Englishman, a regular army officer with a high regard for his own abilities, which he had earned. For all his braggadocio he was intensely human, and he made friends easily. He did not feel the usual British officer's need to look down his nose at the country bumpkins with whom he was often surrounded. He did not treat all civilians as if they were naughty children. And—he knew his water craft.

Bradstreet had been in charge of the bateaux and whaleboats on the expedition to Ticonderoga, and also of the boatmen, civilians who were not overly tolerant of military

The Surrender of Louisbourg

supervision. He had done a good job. It was largely because of his exertions that the beginnings of a panic were checked and the boats kept together until all frightened retreaters could get into them. Now he was after General Abercromby, in the quiet of upper Lake George, to permit him to make a lightning raid on Fort Frontenac at the eastern end of Lake Ontario near the entrance to the St. Lawrence.[34] The French would not expect such a raid, he argued.

Such a stroke had been part of the original plan, but its execution was to be put off until Ticonderoga had been taken and the fort there properly restored and garrisoned. Bradstreet, a man hard to resist, contended that it still could be made. Even less now, was his point, after that bloody repulse, would the French expect it.

Old Abbie-Pamby wavered. He was afraid to split his force, for he seems to have thought that the French would counterattack, something the French were much too weak to do. At last the General gave in, and Bradstreet, temporarily invested with the "in America" rank of lieutenant colonel, took 123 bateaux and all 90 of the whaleboats and started up the valley of the Mohawk August 12.

That raid was a model, a whirlwind. Bradstreet drove the men mercilessly, and he managed to get them up the river, over the Great Carrying Place,[35] across Lake Oneida to the Oswego River, down past the fort Montcalm had razed two years ago, and out into Lake Ontario, with some aid from Chief Red Head and a few of his Onondagas.

The whaleboats, originally purchased at Nantucket and points along Cape Cod, did very well in Lake Ontario so far from home. The surprise was complete.

Frontenac was a strong *looking* place, made largely of stone; but it was brittle, and badly put together, and it shivered every time a cannon in it was fired. It must have been built largely to impress the Indians, nobody ever supposing that the English and provincials would dare to get more than 200 miles from their nearest base, now that Oswego was gone. There were 60-odd cannons in the place, and 16 mortars, and 110 men, together with vast supplies of furs and food. In addition, the invaders took over the entire Lake Ontario "navy," two gunboats and a smattering of smaller craft. These they filled with loot—they had much more than they could possibly carry away—and towed them out to deep water and burned them.

The loot that they *could* carry, mostly furs, blankets, and Indian gifts, was by previous agreement divided equally among the civilians and militiamen, once they were safely back at the Great Carrying Place.

Bradstreet had cut the French supply line to the Ohio, dealt a stunning blow to the French trade with the western Indians, destroyed the French fleet in the Great Lakes, all this inside six weeks and without losing a man. He would go far, that one.[36]

A less exciting stroke, though an equally telling one, was conducted by Brigadier General John Forbes, a grizzled Scot of forty-nine who had been senior staff officer under Loudoun, and who was to complete the task that Braddock left unfinished. Fort Duquesne would wither on the vine as a result of Bradstreet's feat, but Bradstreet had not even started out, or got Abercromby's permission to go, at the time that Forbes was organizing *his* expedition.

As there had been with Braddock, only much more bitterly, there was wrangling between Virginia and Pennsylvania as to the route to be taken. If Duquesne fell, and it was generally assumed that it would, this time, and that the British would rebuild it, it would make a great deal of difference, hard money difference, in which state the "official" supply route started.

Colonel Byrd and Colonel Washington were especially vociferous in their insistence upon the Virginia route, and no mention was made of their holdings in the Ohio Company.

George Washington raising the British flag at Fort Duquesne

Washington indeed carried resistance almost to the point of insubordination, and though he was to go on the expedition he went ungraciously, as a grumpy guest rather than as a guide.

They pointed out that the Braddock route from Virginia was shorter and that most of the work on it already had been done. The bridges that Braddock had built, for example, still stood, the trees he had felled still were down.

Nevertheless Forbes opted for the Pennsylvania route, which would provide better supplies and more wagons and horses.

Instead of the dash that Braddock had tried, the plan was to take it leg by leg, establishing bases as they went along. Before they started they summoned a powwow of Indians, chiefly Delawares and Susquehannas, at Easton, Pennsylvania, where they solemnly promised the assembled braves that Great Britain wanted no land and would *take* no land the other side of the mountains; and the savages, the fools, believed this.

The going, especially in the western mountains, was hard, and Forbes, a sick man, had to be carried in a litter between two horses; but though he cursed prodigiously he stuck to it.

He was lucky in his second-in-command, Lieutenant Colonel Henry Bouquet, a Swiss, who headed the 60th Royal Americans, which was made up largely of German emigrants to Pennsylvania. Bouquet never lost his temper, even when his chief was in a rage, which was much of the time.

When November arrived, with the first breath of winter, they were almost ready to call it a season and to settle on the banks of the Loyalhanna; but the weather held, and was open, and so they pushed on a little farther—until soon their scouts heard the sounds for which Braddock's officers had listened in vain, the explosions that told that the French were blowing up their fort.

The British immediately set about rebuilding the place, and they renamed it Fort Pitt after the Great Commoner. The town that soon grew up around it was called Pittsburgh, as it still is.

General Forbes died soon afterward in Philadelphia, still short of fifty but worn out.

11

Consternation in Canada

THERE WAS CONSTERNATION in Canada. As always, the greatest handicap was the lack of manpower. The first Canadians, after the Indians, were largely from the northwestern part of France—Normandy, Anjou, Poitou, Maine. They were good men, solid, stolid, hard workers; but they were never numerous. They multiplied, but not sensationally, and there were never many women. Even in times of peace it was difficult to talk Frenchmen into crossing the sea to settle in a new land; and in times of war it was impossible.

The Canadians were utterly dependent upon France, the only nation with which they were permitted to deal. They made nothing, and exported only furs.

Every male resident was subject to service in the militia. There was no question of beating the drum for volunteers, as in the English colonies. But they were scattered; and they were not fond of fighting, for their thoughts were on the condition of their crops back home. Under Montcalm and Governor Vaudreuil an effort was made to integrate these militia units with regular troops, but this only resulted in lowering the morale of the regulars, for the militiamen, excellent in the woods, simply could not grasp conventional battlefield practices: for one thing, they insisted upon lying down to reload.

Moreover, there were never many regulars. The British Navy saw to that. There was only one entrance to New France, and that was by way of the St. Lawrence River, an entrance the British Navy zealously watched.

The ministers in Paris never did realize the importance of France's American colonies, and they were understandably reluctant to send overseas soldiers who might not get there, soldiers who were needed at home, on the battlefields of Europe, in the long fight against Frederick the Great. "After all," the minister of war put it to Montcalm's messenger, Louis-Antoine de Bougainville, "when the mansion is on fire one does not think of protecting the stable." To which Bougainville retorted that at least nobody could accuse Monsieur le Ministre of talking like a horse.

This Bougainville was an extraordinarily gifted young man. He was short and fat and suffered from asthma, and he was good company. He had written a paper on integral calculus that won him election to the British Royal Society. He had served in the suite of the French ambassador to the Court of St. James's, and his English was impeccable. Now he was a colonel of regulars, at twenty-nine, and close to Montcalm, who had dispatched him to France to plead for reinforcements and a clearer definition of his own, Montcalm's, power. The marquis himself, though he longed for another sight of his château at Candiac, his wife and dear children, his chestnut grove, his mulberry trees, could not spare the time to return to France.

Bougainville was industrious. He saw sundry ministers, saw the King, and, most important of all, saw Mme. de Pompadour. He got sympathy and some honors, which cost nothing. He himself was made a brigadier and a Chevalier de St. Louis; Governor Vaudreuil was granted the Grand Cross de St. Louis, which Bougainville should take back to him;

François Gaston de Lévis, Montcalm's second-in-command, was raised to major general; and the marquis himself (who would have dearly loved to be a marshal) was made a lieutenant general. But of troops there were precious few. Montcalm and Vaudreuil must do the best they could with what they had.

This was crushing news, for Pitt's intentions were plain. The Great Commoner had every detail of the 1759 campaign planned—excepting how to pay for it—and he made no secret of where the pressure would be applied. The scanty shivering French at Quebec and Montreal, and at Trois Rivières, which is about halfway between the two, could expect attack from the east, up the St. Lawrence; from the south, from New York; and from the west, down the St. Lawrence, now that England had control of Lake Ontario.

The Gascon Montcalm, for all his native exuberance, feared the worst. And if the worst came, and he was forced out of the St. Lawrence valley, he planned to retreat by way of the Mississippi to New Orleans. He braced himself, and waited.

Winters in Canada traditionally were long and hard, and with an invasion due in the spring this one of 1758–1759 seemed hardest and longest of them all. The crops had been poor, chiefly because the farmers had been obliged to spend so much time in the militia on active service. The colonial government, almost unbelievably corrupt, had a monopoly on all imports, and prices, always high, were never higher. Flour, to name but one, sold for 200 francs a barrel. Additionally, Wolfe's calculated depredations of the Gulf of St. Lawrence villages had considerably cut down the supply of fish.

The distance from Quebec to the open sea is about 700 miles, and those who had the defense of New France on their hands appeared to believe that the river itself was their mightiest defense against attack from the east. The St. Lawrence, closed by ice from October to April, is a wide river and not snaky, but it held some dangerous uncharted shoals and many a treacherous current. Taking large ships up to Quebec was always a business fraught with risk even for the finest French pilots—and no other pilots had been permitted to learn the secrets of this river. The St. Lawrence had not been fortified at any point below the city of Quebec itself; but warships, because of their heavy defensive timbers and also because of their great weight of guns, drew more water than ordinary sailing vessels, and it seemed unlikely to those in command that *any* British naval vessel would get through and certainly not *many* would. Even when Bougainville had returned from France, early in May, with a warning from the minister of war that an enormous expedition to be under the command of "le General Wolf" was being fitted out for a descent upon Quebec, the city fathers were not unduly flustered.

An attack from upriver seemed equally unlikely, if only because it would mean that the English would have to venture so far from their base.

The George-Champlain-Richelieu route looked the most dangerous, and it was known that another huge expedition was being readied for New York. To nobody's amazement General Abercromby had been replaced as commander in chief by General Amherst, who was amassing artillery pieces and supplies.

Nevertheless the French commander at Ticonderoga, Bourlamaque, a brigadier, had not been reinforced, and his orders were to fall back at the approach of Amherst lest he lose his whole army in one fight. Bourlamaque was to hold at all costs Ile aux Noix, a naturally strong place at the northern tip of Lake Champlain near the head of the Richelieu River.

The orders to Bourlamaque came from Montcalm, not from Governor-General Vaudreuil, a vain, bigoted man, intensely jealous of the marquis. Among the papers Bougainville had brought back was an order definitely commanding the governor-general to defer to the Marquis de Montcalm in all military matters. This would help, if it had not come too late. It made the governor furious, though he was still a power in military affairs in Canada, for he controlled the militia and all the Indians.

Ils ne passerons pas might have been the slogan of the residents of New France in that year of 1759. There was nothing in any of their plans and preparations that was not defensive. The best they could hope to do was hang on.

It might be said of Jeffrey Amherst that what he was most famous for was taking his time. He was to have more than 16,000 men, about half provincials and half regulars, the provincials largely from New England and New Jersey, when he took over active command at headquarters in New York City, but almost immediately he weakened that force by telling off two brigadiers, Prideaux and Stanwix, to lead expeditions to the west. Stanwix was to bolster up the garrison at Fort Pitt, which he did. Prideaux was to rebuild Fort Oswego and then go on and take Fort Niagara near the foot of the river of that name. Prideaux accomplished both parts of his task, though he lost his life in doing so because of the accidental firing of one of his own cannons.

It must be assumed that when Amherst authorized these side-thrusts he was acting under orders, for they were not orthodox moves. If he had kept his full force intact, he might well have crashed through all the French defenses to reach the St. Lawrence and Quebec in time greatly to strengthen and to take command of Wolfe's up-the-river force. Oswego, Pittsburgh, and Fort Niagara were no good to the British without Quebec, and *with* Quebec Niagara would have fallen of its own accord, while Pittsburgh and Oswego could not even have been threatened.

It was late in June before Amherst started north. He had then about 11,000 men. Bourlamaque, waiting for him at Ticonderoga, had fewer than 4,000.

Amherst had established a large base camp near Albany,[37] and from there in due time he ambled north to the head of Lake George, where he paused to rebuild Fort William Henry, or rather to build a new fort near there with what remained of William Henry. He was a great hand for building forts. He had faith in them.

From afar, by means of spies, he studied his real objective, Fort Carillon.[38] However, he did not move in that direction until the end of July. It was the 26th when he ground to a halt before the place.

It was strangely quiet. No smoke stood up from the kitchens, no sentries paced the wall, and the log breastwork that had given so much trouble to Abercromby's men the previous summer was deserted. Amherst's troops occupied that breastwork in, as it were, reverse; but they continued warily to watch the fort itself. The General might have known that Bourlamaque already had evacuated the place, but he must have assumed that at least a rear guard would be left behind, and he was no man to assault even a rear guard unless he had softened it first by a thorough bombardment. He ordered up his artillery.

Then three French deserters appeared, furtive fellows, who declared that the post really was empty, for the rear guard, some 400 men under Colonel Hebecourt, had cleared out several hours ago. If Amherst had moved just a little less slowly he could have scooped up this package.

A long hidden fuse leading to a magazine had been left lighted, the deserters said. Amherst promptly offered 100 gold guineas out of his own purse to the man who would go back into the fort and stamp out that fuse. Whether they were scared or whether they really didn't know, all three refused.

Then there was nothing to do but wait for the bang, as they stayed safely behind the breastwork. They waited a long

while, and they were beginning to wonder whether those deserters had not been acting under orders, when it happened.

The whole world seemed to be torn apart. Flames leapt
up, debris pattered down. Nobody had ever heard such a
loud noise.

Soon there were smaller but still angry explosions as the
cannons left overloaded and primed went off, one by one,
like gigantic firecrackers. It was not until after dawn that
anybody ventured to approach the post.

Not the whole fort, as they had supposed, but only one
bastion had been destroyed. However, the exploding cannons and the fires that had been started did much to damage
the rest.

General Amherst ordered that it be rebuilt on an enlarged scale, and he renamed it Fort Ticonderoga. Then he
moved to nearby Crown Point, also deserted, and he started
to rebuild *that*.

These jobs, which took him all the rest of the summer
and all of the fall, were very expensive and caused a lot of
grumbling at home, where taxes skyrocketed. The forts never
were finished.

There was another and more rational reason that Amherst did not pursue Bourlamaque. The French had four
small but well-gunned boats in Lake Champlain, and until
he got rid of these he would not dare to try to carry his men
and guns and supplies the whole length of the lake to Ile aux
Noix. Amherst then built three rather larger gunboats, which
sank or otherwise demolished the French fleet almost without
the firing of a shot. But by that time it was November, too
late for any real action. The push north would have to wait
until the next year.

Amherst left large garrisons at his various building sites
and himself went to Albany. He wanted to get back to his
headquarters in New York City, and instead of going in the

usual manner, by sloop, he decided just for the hell of it to walk. He had himself rowed across the river and started south on foot. The distance was about 150 miles. He left December 5 and got there December 11, which means that he did some heavy legging. It was said to be the only time that he ever did go fast.

12

To Take a Continent

As the winters in Canada were long, so the campaigning season was short. Whatever Wolfe was going to do about the seizure of Quebec—the very heart of New France—would have to be done before the end of September. After that the Royal Navy could not support him directly.

It was not much time in which to take a continent.

His was one expedition, by God, that was going to get started on time—even, conceivably, ahead of time. In fact, it left Spithead February 17, some 200 ships of the line, frigates, sloops of war, and transports. Wolfe had been promised 12,000 troops, but even with the ones he was to pick up in America he had only about 8,600. In addition, there were 13,500 sailors and marines in charge of Admiral Sir Charles Saunders, a quiet man who got things done. Of him, Horace Walpole said, "No man said less, or deserved more." The thirty-two-year-old commander in chief himself lay below suffering from seasickness the whole way.

When they arrived at Louisbourg, which was to have been their rendezvous, they found the bay still blocked with ice, so they went around to Halifax instead, except that

Admiral Durell with 10 vessels was sent to watch the mouth of the St. Lawrence and prevent French supply ships from getting in, while Admiral Holmes went to New York for more troops.

Durell nabbed only three of the supply ships, eight others slipping past him, and later another three got by and went up the river. But that was all, and it was a drop in the bucket.

The advance guard got to Bec on the lower St. Lawrence May 23, having encountered no difficulties. A little farther up, at Ile aux Coudres, they stopped for pilots, as was the custom. Ahead lay the trickiest stretch of river, the Traverse, between Cape Tourmente and the lower end of the long Ile d'Orleans just below the city of Quebec itself. The French were saying that no English vessel ever would get through the Traverse. Durell solved that problem very easily. He had his vessels fly French flags, a legitimate *ruse de guerre* at that time, and when pilots came out in their canoes he quietly kidnapped them and warned them that if they allowed a single vessel to go aground they would pay for it with their lives. They spluttered, some shrilly, but perforce they obeyed; and when he was through with them he sent them back to the rest of the fleet.

By June 27 the last of them had dropped hook off the Ile d'Orleans. The English had done the impossible, and without loss of a man.

Quebec, indeed all of Canada, now was completely sealed off.

Quebec, as all the world knows, is a city of savage beauty built on a rock. It was not well fortified,[39] but its natural defenses were great. It is situated about 300 miles from the mouth of the St. Lawrence River, and about twice that distance from the open Atlantic. It is 180 miles downriver from Montreal.

The name means, in Algonquin, "strait" or "narrow place." The river until this point had been very wide—twelve to fourteen miles wide at some places—but here it pinches until it is only about three quarters of a mile across. This is really a tidal estuary, and some of the tides are strong.

Quebec was never impregnable, though it might look that way. It had fallen in 1629 to Sir David Kirke, but was restored to France by the Treaty of St. Germain-en-Laye. In 1690 Sir William Phips, governor of the Massachusetts Bay Colony, attacked it with a fleet from New England, but was beaten off by Governor Frontenac. In 1711, in the course of Queen Anne's War, Sir Hovenden Walker made a try, but thanks to a terrible storm that sank several of his vessels, disabling others, he never did get out of the Gulf of St. Lawrence and into the river proper.

The city consists of an Upper Town and a Lower Town, the former some 250 feet above the surface of the St. Lawrence, the latter, chiefly commercial, a labyrinth of narrow streets down almost at the level of the river. This river formed one side of what amounted to a rough triangle. Another side, to the east, was formed by the St. Charles, a rivulet as compared with the majestic St. Lawrence, but a turbulent rivulet with steep banks, a rivulet that could not be forded for some five miles in from the big river. The French had spanned the St. Charles with a bridge of boats, which could easily have been destroyed in an emergency, and which in any case was almost a mile from the St. Lawrence and out of range of the guns of any warship anchored there, for shoal water would keep such ships a good half-mile off the mouth of the St. Charles.

It was the third side of the triangle that was its weakness. This was a flat plateau called the Plains of Abraham after its original owner, a pilot named Abraham Martin, usually known as Maître Abraham. This side of the city had been walled; but the walls, though they were high, were, like the two gates, not strong: they would not have lasted long against any well-manned battery.

Montcalm's first thought had been to place most of his

men on the Plains of Abraham, making it into a fortified camp to protect the weak side, but he later decided to establish such a camp instead at Beaufort, a level stretch just downriver from Quebec, between the St. Charles and Montmorency rivers. The Montmorency was an even smaller stream than the St. Charles but every bit as tumultuous, and its mouth was blocked by a waterfall so that it could not be ascended in boats from the St. Lawrence.

This encampment Montcalm had caused to be guarded by eight miles of trenches. It was an extremely strong spot, and he had no intention of letting anything lure him out of it. "The old fox," Wolfe was to call him, admiringly.

Wolfe might have expected as much. He knew, at least in a general way, the nature of the city of Quebec and its surroundings, and he must already have given thought to what *he*, as a general, would have done to protect it, if the positions had been reversed. The French always had been jealous of New France, allowing no Huguenots there, no foreigners, an attitude much like that of the Spaniards in *their* closed colonies farther south. But there were peepholes in this enswathement. For one, Major Patrick Mackeller, a British Army engineer who had been captured at Oswego, and who had spent more than a year at Quebec while waiting to be exchanged, had made a careful map of the city and its environs, so far as he had been permitted to view them; and this map was in Wolfe's possession.

Though the French had professed to believe that no considerable part of the British fleet would get as far up the river as the Ile d'Orleans, nevertheless they had made preparations to burn whatever units *did* get there. Eight fire ships, soaked in oil and crammed with combustibles, had been lashed together. One of these had gone off prematurely. The others were sent against the British fleet near the upriver end of the long island the second night after it had anchored there—that is, the night of June 28. Just what went wrong probably never will be known, but the fire ships burst into flame much too soon. The westernmost British warship cut her cables and ran for it, but the others had plenty of time to send out longboat crews who coolly towed the blazing, exploding ships out of harm's way, all without the loss of a man. The show had been spectacular, but of no avail. It was said to have cost Louis XV a good round 1,000,000 gold livres, much of it in the form of army contractors' graft.

All the same, the French made immediate preparations for a second such attack.

The French had made no move to hold the Ile d'Orleans but had withdrawn their few small posts there as soon as the British arrived. Wolfe occupied the western end of the island at first, and then he made his main camp on the northern bank of the St. Lawrence just below the Montmorency. Parts of this camp were less than a mile from parts of Montcalm's camp at Beaufort, but there was no fighting there, for the Montmorency intervened.

The distance between the St. Charles and the Montmorency rivers—the width, that is, of Montcalm's entrenched camp—was about six miles.

The marquis' plans continued to be defensive. He only wished to hold on, to keep his army in existence, and he prayed that Bourlamaque could hold out against Amherst in New York. If by any chance Quebec should be taken by assault and all of his supplies taken with it, then the game would be up, and the rest of New France would fall like a ripe plum into the lap of the British. If, however, the marquis and any considerable part of his army could escape from such a seizure—and they could expect to escape only upriver, since the hinterland would not support them and the St. Lawrence below Quebec already was firmly in the hands of the Royal Navy—they would need some large source of supplies, particularly of food, if they expected even to hold together, even to retreat. It was for this reason that Montcalm was keeping in Quebec only about enough food to feed his men from day to day. The rest, the great bulk of the stores, was kept at various points up the river, most of it in Montreal, 180 miles away. There were roads between Montreal and Quebec, but they were execrable. Easily the best way to move supplies down to the capital was by boat. If the British Navy ever ran the gauntlet of the Upper Town batteries to get into the river above Quebec, it would be possible to move those supplies only by night, which would be both difficult and dangerous. Montcalm at first believed that the British Navy would never be able to do this, not only because of the cannons but also because of the tides, which were very tricky at this point. He was soon disillusioned. Within a few days sloops, frigates, and ships of the line were easily running past the Upper Town batteries. It was alarming. If a landing ever was made there, and held, Montcalm's supply line was cut, and he would be forced to come out of his prepared position and give battle. This he feared to do. He had more men, but the British, he knew, from the point of view of "the art of war" were better men, much better. Their discipline was better. And they had a navy behind them.

Montcalm already had sent Bougainville with 1,600 troops to guard the shore of the north bank between Quebec and Pointe aux Trembles, 22 miles upriver. Now he increased this force to 2,000, at the same time imploring his young friend to be always on the alert.[40]

Cape Diamond, 333 feet above the surface of the St. Lawrence, and just slightly upriver from the city itself, was the highest point anywhere on the north bank. It was not fortified. It made a good observation post, but the kind of cannons available to General Montcalm would have served no purpose there. To take Cape Diamond anyway an enemy would first have to take the Upper Town itself.

That Cape Diamond was not fortified, then, is easily understood. It is not so easy to see why Point Lévis, just across the river from Quebec on the south bank, should have been left without any protection. Whatever the reason, it was a happy chance for Wolfe, who took advantage of it, occupying Lévis as one of his first moves. He brought up some heavy guns, and soon he had the whole city, Lower Town and Upper Town alike, under bombardment.

This set many buildings afire, including the hospital, but it did nothing toward taking the city. Such civilians as were not killed in the first bombardment quit the Lower Town and the Upper Town too, and found refuge in the surrounding countryside, or, more often, in one of the villages upriver. Wolfe went on lambasting the ruin.

The weeks frittered by. There was seldom even any skirmishing. Montcalm sat tight.

In the beginning Wolfe had issued a cheery proclamation addressed to the inhabitants of the countryside, promising them that they would be well treated if only they respected the authority of the invaders, but warning them that if they took sides in the present conflict they must be treated as enemies. He never did have any real trouble with the natives, though they were scarcely friendly, but soon he became edgy, suspecting things. He sent out squads instructed to burn everything but the churches and to confiscate all grain and livestock and in fact anything edible. In a few cases the *habitants* themselves were mistreated, but most of them got out of the way before the redcoats arrived. It was estimated that more than 1,400 farm buildings were burned to the ground in this campaign, and the confiscations undoubtedly did do something to sharpen Montcalm's food problem.

All this time the commander in chief wore a sour expression, for he was never well, never had been well. His digestion was delicate, to say the least of it, and he suffered from sundry skin afflictions. Also, he was given to bouts of palsy. It has been deduced by a physician that he suffered all his life from tuberculosis of the kidneys, which would mean that he was never really free of pain.[41] He confided in no one, but glowered alone.

The night of July 27–28 the French tried their fire-ship tactic again, on an even larger scale. It was even more emphatically a failure, thanks to the swiftness and courage with which sailors in small boats hauled the flaming vessels and rafts aside. Once again, it was a splendid show; but nobody was hurt. For their services that night the members of the various boat crews were given half a pint of brandy apiece. Probably it was confiscated stuff. The ordinary R.N. issue liquor was rum.

The last day of that month Wolfe launched his attack on Montcalm's lines between the Montmorency and the St. Charles, somewhat nearer to the former, the falls.

He had brought with him from Louisbourg and Halifax ten regular line battalions, one small provisional battalion formed from the grenadier companies of three battalions left at Louisbourg, three companies of the Royal Regiment of Artillery, and four, and, a little later, two more companies of American Rangers. The grenadiers, crack troops, were to lead the charge.

He might have seen or thought that he saw a weakness in the French lines of entrenchment. It could have been a good plan, but certainly it was not well executed.

Either the grenadiers were so excited that they "jumped the gun," which was not likely, or else somebody gave the wrong order or gave the right order at the wrong time. Anyway, the grenadiers, with bayonets fixed, started up the slope alone, before the companies that were supposed to support them were in position. They were met by a withering fire and dropped right and left. They tried to rally, and were mowed down again.

Then there came, suddenly, dramatically, a summer thunderstorm. It was a particularly fierce one. Torrents fell.

Lightning flashed. The slope in seconds became a sea of mud. The grenadiers stumbled down to the shore, leaving their dead and wounded; and immediately afterward Indians came slithering out of the trenches and went to work with their scalping knives in full view of those on both sides. It was a gruesome sight.[42]

The so-called Battle of Montmorency might better be called the Massacre of Montmorency. The French casualties were next to nothing; the French had never left their trenches. The British, who had not taken a square foot of ground, lost 443 killed, wounded, and missing, including one colonel, eight captains, 21 lieutenants, and three ensigns.

The French, jubilant, had a celebration, a fete. They assumed that after such a smashing defeat the British would fall down the river, abandoning the siege.

General Wolfe, upset, took to his bed. A great gloom fell upon the British camp.

13

How to Outfox a Fox

THE COMMANDER IN CHIEF had three brigadiers, Robert Monckton, George Townshend, and James Murray, all young men; and though he resented Townshend's acidulous pencil—the man had a habit of caricaturing the commander in chief—on the whole he got along well enough with them, largely because he stayed aloof. He had not once asked their advice.

All three, though without titles of their own, were the sons of peers, whereas Wolfe had a middle-class background. This might have had something to do with the coolness. Though they seldom mention such things, Englishmen think about them.

When three days had passed with no word from the sickroom, the terrible rumor spread that the commander in chief had died. Panic was just around the corner, for the men had illimitable faith in their leader. It was said that the lesser generals were keeping the death a secret, for fear that the news would cause the army to disintegrate. Other things like this were said.

Wolfe himself dispelled these rumors on the fourth day when he appeared, pale and drawn, in public. The fever had passed, though his eyes still held an unnatural brightness.

He did not summon Murray, Townshend, and Monckton into conference, but he did write to them, suggesting, for the first time, that they study the situation and advise him as to what they thought the next move should be.

There were several courses open to Wolfe.

He could hook far around to the rear of the French camp at Beaufort, threatening to debouch upon the Plains of Abraham unless the French came out of their entrenchments to block him. That would take him a long way from his base, a long way from the navy, and it would leave him open to a counterattack at Montmorency that might cut him off from the river. Moreover, he had scouted the upper Montmorency with such a move in mind, and had failed to find a suitable ford.

He could have another try at the frontal attack up the slope to the Beaufort camp, but the remembrance of what had happened to the grenadiers discouraged that idea.

He could listen to those who urged him to occupy the Lower Town. This would not be an expensive operation. But what would it get him? The navy had already closed Quebec to all commerce downriver, closed it, that is, as a port. Occupation of the Lower Town would only mean possession of buildings already largely pounded to rubble by the guns at Point Lévis. There would be no supplies there to seize, no guns or ammunition, probably no soldiers. And the Upper Town, which is what counted, would be as far away as ever, for the paths between them were few, narrow, and exceedingly steep, so that a handful of men above could keep a whole army from getting up.

Already some of the high navy men—Wolfe never trusted the navy—were talking about dropping down the St. Lawrence, in order to play it safe. The possibility of being frozen in for the winter was a nightmare to them. It would not only be a disaster in itself: it would virtually halve the Royal Navy, leaving the French superior at sea. September was the month they had most often mentioned in the past, but now they were getting nervous about Wolfe's lack of activity and were openly wondering whether an even earlier departure might not be advisable. It was already August.

Wolfe could not tell the Royal Navy what to do and what not to do. They were cooperative; they could and did help; but understandably they thought of their own affairs first.

Of one thing he was certain: he would never call the whole business off and creep back to England with, figuratively, his tail between his legs. This possibility he could not even contemplate.

If the navy did leave him, he thought of dropping down the river as far as Ile aux Coudres, a pilot station about 60 miles away, and holing up there for the winter, to renew the siege as early in the spring as he could be resupplied. It was a wild thought, but anything was better than the prospect of going home empty-handed.

At this juncture his brigadiers, prodded, came up with still another possible plan. Why not, they asked, move all or most of the troops to the south bank of the river, ceasing to threaten the too-strong camp at Beaufort, and gradually shift them upstream until they could all be moved at once across the St. Lawrence to some weak spot soon to be selected? Then, if they could make the move in force, they would be between Montcalm and his supplies, and he would *have* to come out.

It is hard to believe that Wolfe had not previously considered such a move, though there is no evidence that he had. It presented some mammoth problems. The men would have to be taken out of the camp on the Montmorency River and transported first to the south bank and later to the north bank again upriver, all this at the risk of a flank attack. Supplies too would have to be so moved. The landing would have to be a large one, for a smallish one could be nipped off by Bougainville's men or men from the camp between the

Montmorency and the St. Charles who would cross the latter stream by the bridge of boats, or by both. Absolute secrecy must be maintained, and the French must be misled as to the place of the all-out attack.

It would be a terrible risk, and one more disaster like that of the last day of July would mean an end to the whole expedition. But what else could he do? He consented to the plan.

He did not agree that the neighborhood of Cap Rouge, about nine miles above Quebec, was the best place for a landing. He wished to get nearer to the city; and the place they at last selected, Anse au Foulon,[43] was only about two miles from the city. The rise at that point—in part a rocky cliff, in part a steep wooded bank—was about 175 feet high. A path could be discerned zigzagging up this slope, but it would surely be defended by some sort of outwork. Men might be able to get up there, but could they haul guns up? They must try.

At first it looked as though Wolfe planned another straight-ahead attack against the Beaufort camp near the Montmorency falls. Soldiers were taken out of camp and brought offshore in transports, their bayonets at the ready; while the navy from a somewhat greater distance bombarded Beaufort as though in a softening-up process. Then, when it would seem that a landing was about to be made, the transports suddenly went instead to Point Lévis, where the men were disembarked.

In this way the camp on the Montmorency was emptied without any loss through lateral attack, and the first step was taken toward a stroke from the west, from upriver.

The Marquis de Montcalm still sturdily believed that the camp at Beaufort was the real target, and that these recent movements had been merely for the purpose of confusement. "The old fox" in effect was being outfoxed.

There followed a series of aquatic movements back and

forth before the Upper Town batteries that must indeed have bewildered French observers. The biggest ships of the line, including Admiral Saunders' flagship, generally maintained their positions before the Beaufort camp, but sloops and frigates and transports scuttled back and forth without any show of reason or plan.

September 8 and 9, for instance, there was a great gathering of war vessels around Pointe aux Trembles, as though a landing was in preparation, but then the troops were all hauled away and taken back to Point Lévis.

Bougainville and his 2,000 were kept busy scampering back and forth between Pointe aux Trembles and Cape Diamond, a distance of more than 20 miles; and they were exhausted.

The Royal Navy was busy. It landed no seamen and lent the army no gunners—Wolfe did not need any more gunners, anyway—but it shuttled back and forth at a dizzying pace. There were some 2,000 marines in the various vessels, and every effort was made to keep them in sight as much as possible. The marines wore red coats very similar to the coats of the army regulars—exactly the same at a slight distance—so that the French observers could never be sure how many soldiers were being moved or why.

Montcalm still clung to the belief that the real attack, if it ever came, would be at Beaufort. He was firmly dug in. Moreover, the news that came from the Champlain area had Bourlamaque retreating to Ile aux Noix, where he too was firmly in place, so that Amherst was refraining from pursuit. All they needed to do was hold on.

The food situation at Beaufort was grim, since supplies were getting past the Royal Navy only in driblets, and for this reason among others the Canadian militiamen, anxious to get back to their farms, were deserting in droves. Many of these deserters were picked up by the British soldiery and questioned by French-speaking officers, and they told a tale of discontent, though not of disintegration.

The British aim, on the other hand, was perfectly guarded. Not a hint slipped out. When the landing at last was made at Anse au Foulon early on the morning of September 13, it came as a complete surprise.

The moon had risen at ten o'clock that night, but it was in its third quarter and did not betray them as they rowed without a sound, without a light, along the north bank of the St. Lawrence, under the beetling cliffs, from Cap Rouge to the little cove of Foulon. They were challenged by a sentry at least once, and there may have been more times, but a quick-witted Highland officer whose French was good responded that they were bringing down supplies, and they were never asked to give the countersign.[44]

By an incredible stroke of luck the word had gone out early that evening, to all sentries along the river, that a large provisions train from Pointe aux Trembles would make its stealthy way just off the north bank that night. Sentries should not challenge too loudly, lest they bring upon this convoy the fire of the Royal Navy. The movement had been postponed, perhaps because of the unusual activity among the naval vessels off Cap Rouge, but this bit of information had not been passed along to the sentries. The Comte de Bougainville had many accomplishments, but as a military manager he was not preeminent.

The first of the British stepped ashore half an hour before the dawn was due.

The forlorn hope consisted of 24 volunteers, all light infantrymen, an experimental corps something like the American Rangers, though by no means as informal, headed by a plump sleepy-eyed young colonel named William Howe, a younger brother of the Lord Howe who had lost his life before Ticonderoga.[45] Not all British Army officers of the time thought that the Germanic rigidity and lack of imagination that characterized European armies was the best possible thing, and some, like Howe, were seeking to modify it. He was interested in the evolvement of the light infantry and the grenadiers, the so-called "flank companies," but especially the light infantry. He was preparing to write a textbook on the subject.

This stretch of shore was scantily defended, not by Bougainville's regulars but by militiamen from the city, militiamen under his command. It was directly in the charge of one Captain Vergor, who had let half of his men go back to their farms along the St. Charles with the proviso that they spend part of their leave taking care of *his* farm as well—against regulations but apparently a common practice at the time. Neither Vergor nor his men were alert. They were quickly overrun, without the firing of a single shot, and the way was cleared for the men below, men who were already climbing.

The first rays of the sun, then, gilded a force on the Plains of Abraham, a force that was rapidly growing.

At the same time, by prearranged signal, all the war vessels downriver opened up with everything they had upon the fortified camp at Beaufort.

The Marquis de Montcalm, who had not had his clothes off for more than a week, was hastily summoned. He could hardly believe his eyes when he saw the scene on the Plains of Abraham. But he knew what it meant: he had to fight.

He called out his men. He sent for guns. He sent for Bougainville.

But he did not wait for Bougainville. The plump young expert on integral calculus had some of the best troops in the French army under him, but he did not get the marquis' message until about nine o'clock and it is not likely that he could have arrived in time to make any difference in the first open battle ever to be fought in North America. For Montcalm attacked at ten.

Montcalm, it would seem, believed that the British were digging in, which was not true. There was almost no food left at Beaufort or in the city, and unless he drove the British away right now, he thought, all would be lost.

The Royal Navy, which in the night just past had performed one of the finest and best synchronized movements in all its long history—an amphibious attack upon enemy territory at night—even brought along two fieldpieces, brass 6-pounders, for Wolfe. These were all the artillery he had or was likely to get for a long while; but Montcalm did not know this.

Nor, after the first two "waves" of boats, would Wolfe get more troops that morning. *He* knew that; but once again, Montcalm did not. It was about eight o'clock when the last men arrived, and Wolfe caused them to be formed in a line parallel to the river, to which they turned their backs. The right wing was extended in the direction of the city. Wolfe, who evidently had expected to be attacked right away, soon swung this line around so that all the men faced the city, the right toward the St. Lawrence, the left toward the St. Charles. Most of the field was bare, but there was a certain amount of sniping and even skirmishing on both wings, where there was some brush.

There were roughly 4,500 on each side. The French had a definite advantage in the matter of artillery.

As was the custom, the French advanced in a straight line abreast, officers with drawn swords seeing to it that they kept in perfect step. They took long, rather slow strides. At a command, some time within 100 yards of the enemy—shots would be wasted at any greater distance—they were to stop, to fire, then to renew that careful stride, reloading as they went. If anybody fell, he was not to be helped at the time (too often in the past a wounded man had been an excuse for five or six friends to get out of the fighting), but simply to be stepped over or around, the ranks to be closed promptly thereafter. Then another measured twenty paces, or thirty, depending upon how the men had been trained; and another stop, another volley. All the time they must remain stiffly upright. Crouching or kneeling was forbidden.

The French did exactly that, or started to. The excite-

A rendering of the death of General James Wolfe before Quebec

ment, the unaccustomed circumstances, were too much for some of the Canadian "fill-ins" who began shooting too soon. What's more, the Canadians after firing would fall to the ground in order to reload. This put the regulars off.

The British, two deep instead of the conventional three, waited unwavering. A few fell. Most of them just stood there with their muskets at the ready.

When the French were near enough, about 40 or 50 yards away, British officers barked orders. The men fired, in perfect unison. Then, without stirring a step either forward or back, they reloaded, and at a command fired again. After the second volley, and with a loud huzzah, they went in with the bayonet.

The French broke and ran.

The battle, the main battle, the conventional battle, had taken only about fifteen minutes.

James Wolfe had been over on the right, and far too much forward for a general officer. Clipped in the right wrist by a ball, he merely wrapped it in a handkerchief and went on watching the fight; but when another ball got him in the chest, he was knocked off his horse. Always the soldier, he had already witnessed the running-away of the French regulars, and on the ground he gasped out an order for Colonel Burton to march Colonel Webb's regiment down to the bridge of boats over the St. Charles in order to cut off Montcalm's retreat.

"Now, God be praised," he said, "I can die in peace," and he did.[46]

Montcalm, a diminutive man but a conspicuous figure in the bright green, gold-fringed coat, on the big black horse, was carried toward the city by the force of a retreat that never did reach the proportions of a rout. He had been hit in the belly, the most painful place, and two aides were holding him in saddle. A little later a surgeon, having examined the wound, warned him that he would not live.

"Good," said the Marquis de Montcalm, "then I will not have to witness the surrender of Quebec."

Nor did he. He was to last until the small hours of the next morning, though he never did fully recover consciousness, and the city was not surrendered until the day after that.

Wolfe's last order never was carried out. There was a great deal of confusion on the field. Monckton should have assumed the command automatically on the death of the major general, but Monckton had himself been wounded and was out of action, and Townshend, the next in seniority, was far over on the left flank, where he was having troubles of his own with a few companies of Canadian militiamen who, from the shelter of bushes, were peppering his men in flank.

The Canadians had not shown up well in the ranks with the regulars, but when they were permitted to fight as they preferred, from behind some kind of cover, they gave a good account of themselves. It was largely the stand of these militiamen on the British left flank that gave the main French army a chance to get back to its fortified camp at Beaufort—and temporary safety. The Canadians, having saved the day, were finally driven off, with heavy losses, by bayonets. They had no bayonets of their own.

Townshend had also to keep a force facing the west, for fear that Bougainville might appear there at any moment. Bougainville actually did come at about twelve noon, but by that time it was all over. Bougainville decided against an attack, and Townshend for his part was only too glad to see him go away, and made no move to pursue.

In this hesitant, uncertain manner there ended the first open-field battle ever fought in America, a battle that was to seal the fate of a continent.

The British kept the field, for what that was worth. The French were back at their base, largely intact, though they had lost their leader.

The British losses were 10 officers and 48 men dead, 37 officers and 535 men wounded. The French losses are not known exactly, but they probably totaled about 1,000.

14

A Thoroughgoing Man

IT HAD BEEN A GLORIOUS YEAR for Great Britain, that year of 1759. Victory tumbled over victory—Gorée, Madras and Masulipatam in India, Minden in Germany, one French fleet beaten by Boscawen off the coast of Portugal, another beaten by Hawke at Quiberon, and now the blasting news of Quebec.

Speeches were made, toasts drunk, salutes fired, and everybody went around congratulating everybody else. It was assumed that this marked the end of the long and bitter fighting, the hideously expensive war.

Not at all in a fit of absentmindedness, as was later to be said, but deliberately and noisily Great Britain had conquered a large part of the world. She was no longer a mere island. She had become an empire.

Those at Quebec itself were not drinking any toasts or shouting any cheers. They were not slapping backs. They had won the capital, and it was a mess. Never had a city been so pounded. The Lower Town, along the water front, was a mere mass of rubble, in places impassable, nowhere habitable. Some buildings stood in the Upper Town, but they stood uncertainly, teetering. There were no creature comforts, and there was not even much food. Quebec, close up, looked like anything but a prize.

Glorious victory? It did not seem so, there. The losses had been about even. The British had taken no outworks. They had taken only a few fieldpieces, and no flags at all; nor had they taken many prisoners.

The French were by no means beaten. The men of the Beaufort camp soon had been able to join Bougainville's men, and so the French army was kept "in being." Nor was it discouraged. The capital of New France had been moved to Montreal, and the French forces, with the exception of those few still at Ile aux Noix, were quartered on or near that island. Under the leadership now of Brigadier General François Gaston de Lévis, a highly emotional man given to gasconading, but a competent soldier, they were already making plans for a counterattack: they would not even wait for the late Canadian spring but would retake Quebec, they boasted, that very winter.

This was exactly what Brigadier Murray feared. Murray was the commanding officer of the British, now that Wolfe was dead and Townshend and the badly wounded Monckton had gone back to London. He was an energetic man, young and imaginative. The soldiers trusted him, and their morale, at least at the beginning of that long terrible winter, was good. They were put to work strengthening the fortifications, which never had been finished, and collecting firewood for the days of intense cold ahead. The firewood assignment was an especially onerous one. There were no trees for many miles, and the men had to trudge both ways on foot, hauling the big logs in sledges on the return trip, for there were almost no oxen or horses left in or near the city.

The first touch of cold—and winter comes early in those parts, as it stays late—resulted in about 150 cases of frostbite. The sentries' spells of duty were cut to three hours, to two, even at last to only one, but still they suffered. The wind had knives in it. The snow was relentless.

Very little loot had been obtained from the smashed-in warehouses of Quebec, but there was at least one large store of French army blankets, and these were distributed among the men, who in most cases cut them into mittens and extra pairs of socks. They kept their faces covered with blanket masks, too, so that they could scarcely recognize one another when they met in the streets. Any kind of garment was permitted, so long as it helped to keep out that implacable cold. No longer were these men members of spit-and-polish regiments.

The nuns of the General Hospital, pitying the Highlanders for their bare legs—the French soldiers called them *les sauvages sans culottes*—cut and sewed many a pair of blanket-wool trousers. For these the recipients were grateful. Scotland, they averred, was never like this.

An enemy even worse than the cold, worse than the French, was scurvy. There was more than a touch of dysentery and the bloody flux that winter in Quebec, but scurvy was almost universal. It might have been expected. No ships would be able to come up the river at least until May, and then they might prove to be French rather than British ships. The surrounding countryside had been stripped of every vestige of fresh food. The men relied entirely upon salted rations.

Scurvy is a malodorous malady. It is also insidious. It saps the strength, yellows the face, fouls the breath, sinks the eyeballs. Men drag themselves around like dispirited ghosts. They groan involuntarily. They vomit a great deal—a greenish, stinking substance.

Scurvy takes a long time; and even when a man is able to resume his place in the ranks he is feeble, bleary, one of an army of "half-starved scorbutic skeletons."

Scurvy also kills. Before that winter was out there were an estimated 700 dead bodies stashed away in snowdrifts just outside the walls of Quebec, where they would remain, frozen, until such time as the ground thawed sufficiently so that they could be buried.

At one time Murray had 2,300 men on the sick list, and no doubt many of those who still staggered on their feet *should* have been there. One third of Murray's whole force was out of action. If Lévis had struck at that time the history of North America would have been changed.

But Lévis did not strike. Despite energetic preparations, he had not been able to get together enough men and supplies.

The French did make one winter stroke, though, when in February they sent a force to occupy Point Lévis just across the river from Quebec, doubtless with the purpose in mind of using it as a jumping-off place—for the river was frozen solid—but the British, still cocky in spite of their sufferings, easily beat off this attack.

Not until April 28 did Lévis come down the river in full strength. He had about twice as many men as Murray was able to muster. Nevertheless Murray, who did not think highly of Quebec's defense walls, went forth to meet him. There were still patches of snow, but the ground had thawed out, and it could be that Murray was afraid that the French would be given time to entrench themselves. If so, he sallied forth for the same reason that Montcalm had sallied forth to his death half a year before, and in the same place.

The first Frenchmen to be met were readily scattered, and they fell back in some confusion into the shadow of Sillery Wood, a swampy low place. This was only the French van, but the Britishers in their exuberance thought that it was the entire army under General Lévis, and once they had it on the run they went after it. They pushed into Sillery Wood, where they learned their mistake.

They were outnumbered, as they were beginning to perceive, and moreover they were being outflanked, the French left hooking around the British right, threatening to cut them off from contact with the city, their base. More-over, the British guns were mired—right up to the hubs of the wheels. Murray ordered a retreat. The men howled in rage, but they did fall back.

There had been two hours of bitter fighting, with the losses about equal on the two sides, but the French kept the field. The British perforce left all their artillery behind— 3 howitzers and 20 brass fieldpieces—and they were lucky to get out with their lives.

Thereafter Lévis, made more prudent, discarded his thought of an immediate attack and ordered instead a siege. The French began to dig in.

May 9 a ship was sighted downriver, the first of the season, a large ship, undoubtedly a warship. Would it be French? Had the French got into the St. Lawrence first? If so, Quebec was doomed, for Lévis, his lines close in now, was ready to attack.

It was not French. It was H.M.S. *Lowestoffe*, flying the red ensign and cramful of fresh supplies. And the next day two other Royal Navy vessels followed it.

The French, no fools, withdrew upriver, in the direction of Montreal. But he would be back, this Monsieur de Lévis. Oh, assuredly he would be back! Brigadier Murray sent to his superior, Amherst, for reinforcements.

General Amherst, upon finishing his long walk of the previous December to New York City, had found waiting for him a great deal of mail, among which was a new set of orders from the Prime Minister, Mr. Pitt. The Prime Minister was known to be deeply disappointed that Amherst had not pushed north from Lake Champlain during the summer just passed, and taken Montreal, winding up the whole op-eration. But his orders were temperate in tone, and unex-pectedly liberal. The General, he stated, would be sent such-and-such reinforcements. Other reinforcements, two full regiments, would be sent to Murray at Quebec, for the Prime

Minister had ordered the vast and mighty Fort Louisbourg to be razed, releasing these.

The General was officially informed that his services of the previous summer would be rewarded by the governorship of Virginia. This alarmed him. He had a pleasant country estate back home in Kent, in the parish of Sevenoaks, where a pleasant wife awaited him, and as soon as this war was over he wished to end his days there. He was still young—he was forty-two—and he certainly did not want to immure himself in the wilds of Virginia. Did this appointment mean that he would actually have to *go* to the place? He was assured that it did not. All he had to do was the usual thing: he would appoint a lieutenant governor to act for him, and he would split the salary and perquisites fifty-fifty with this man, who would do all the work. His half share would still come to £1,500 a year, he was told.[47] On these terms he accepted the governorship.

His mind at rest, then, he turned to the task of crushing New France. It was the kind of work he enjoyed.

It had been left to his discretion whether he should strike Montreal upriver from Quebec, downriver from Lake Ontario, or from the south by means of the Lake George-Lake Champlain-Richelieu River route. A thoroughgoing man, he decided to do all three.

Murray at Quebec, reinforced from Louisbourg, would ascend the river. A Colonel Haviland, raised to a brigadiership for the occasion, would lead the northward strike through Lake Champlain. Amherst himself would take an army up the Mohawk, overland to Lake Ontario, and down the St. Lawrence to Montreal, a side the French had failed to fortify because they believed that the upper river with its angry rapids—the Cedars, the Buisson, the Cascades, others—was impassable by any large military force.

In a wilderness country where the question was not so much how to fight an enemy as how to get at him, this was the epitome of boldness. It would depend upon perfect timing.[48] Amherst, a man devoted to detail, spent all winter planning it at his headquarters in New York City, an old stone house in the fort down at the tip of the Battery.

A last-minute complication was raised by the Cherokees, who went on the warpath. It was necessary that Amherst, as commander in chief in North America, send a punitive expedition into the western part of South Carolina to quell them. He could hardly expect much militia support if he did not, for the militiamen, fearful that other tribes would follow the lead of the Cherokees until the whole frontier was aflame, understandably would elect to stay home. The militias were undependable enough at best. The colonial assemblies even then were discussing how much of their respective quotas they would fill; and they would take a long time at this.

Amherst told off two of his crack regiments, the 1st Royals and Montgomery's Highlanders, 1,300 men in all, to put down the Cherokees. This they did, and did well. They suffered some 80 casualties, but the Cherokees were no longer a real fighting force, and confidence had been restored all up and down the frontier, the doubts raised by the Braddock fiasco being wiped out.

The Montgomery Highlanders and the 1st Royals, however, did not get in on the much more glorious wheeling movement against Montreal.

That went off perfectly. Haviland, with about 3,400 troops from the neighborhood of Crown Point, easily drove a badly weakened Bougainville out of Ile aux Noix, and pushed on toward the new capital.

Murray took 1,700 men out of the 2,200 he had left at Quebec and sailed up the river, bypassing a French fort.

Amherst himself did not have things so easy. He had some 10,000 men under him, but he lost 84 of them at the Cascades rapids, besides 40-odd boats and some supplies.

Then he allowed himself to be held up for five days at Fort
Lévis, the only French stronghold in that part of the river.
He could easily have bypassed Fort Lévis, but he paused
to batter it to pieces, for he was not a man to leave behind
him any undone jobs.

The Iroquois had responded well to Sir William Johnson's appeal. Of late they had been behaving coolly toward
the English, though they had refused even to flirt with the
French; but now they seemed to sense which way the war
was going, and they turned out to the number of 1,300. More
than half of these, however, were women and children, and
Amherst, faced with the necessity of feeding them all—and
they were voracious eaters—was dismayed. Nevertheless, he
pushed on.

At Fort Lévis he was to have trouble with these Indians.
They wanted of course to scalp the prisoners and the French
dead, and this Amherst sternly forbade. He had the dead
buried secretly. But the Iroquois, furious, learned where the
place was and dug up the corpses and scalped *them*. After
this feat of arms about three-quarters of them deserted,
turning back toward Lake Ontario. Amherst was not sorry to
see them go, though he must have regretted that they stole
so many boats when they did so.

All the same, he arrived at the island of Montreal on the
date set, August 29. And so did Haviland. And so did Murray.
It was a masterpiece of the military art, that operation.[49]

There were 2,500 French soldiers in Montreal, virtually
all regulars, for the militia for the most part had deserted.
These were the last in the land; nor could any more be expected, for the Royal Navy controlled the St. Lawrence River.

There were 17,000 English on three sides, the fourth
side being the river.

Montreal was surrounded by a low stone wall, but this
had been designed only to keep out Indians and would be
that much cardboard before such field artillery as Amherst
had in his command.

MAJOR GENERAL JEFFERY AMHERST

Jeffery Amherst took his time, as he always did. He got all his cannons into position, and saw to it that they were supplied with powder and ball. He gave orders for his three gunboats to stand by and prevent any possible escape by water. He formed his foot soldiers into line of battle, with a proper reserve to back them.

Then Colonel Bougainville rode out, a melancholy figure flanked by two aides, one of whom held a white flag. General Amherst received him in person.

The governor of New France, De Vaudreuil, was making an extraordinary suggestion. He proposed that both sides declare a one-month armistice. He hastened to explain, through young Bougainville, that his reason for this suggestion was that he had heard—he did not say through what channels—that the statesmen at home, in both countries, were right on the edge of putting through a peace treaty.

(Whether Vaudreuil really believed this we do not know. There had been no peace move of any sort in Europe up until this time.)

Amherst, being a gentleman, refrained from snickering; but he made himself clear:

"Tell Monsieur de Vaudreuil that I have come to take Canada, and I will take nothing less."

The governor was given a whole afternoon in which to make out a list of the conditions under which he would surrender. He did this, and it was a very long list. Not a shot was fired, but the men stood ready.

General Amherst read the list from beginning to end, agreeing to some clauses, vetoing others. One thing he was careful to emphasize: the French, because of the barbarous way in which from time to time they had conducted the war—he probably had the Fort William Henry massacre in mind, though this was not mentioned—should not be permitted honors of war. He was firm on this point.

It meant a lot to a soldier. In the French camp General de Lévis fumed and spluttered about fighting to the last man. But De Vaudreuil had better sense. He agreed.

The French did burn their regimental colors in advance, an act of monumental pettiness, a sneaky act. They explained that there *were* no regimental colors, that they had lost them. Amherst pretended to believe this.

Thus was New France lost, 9 September 1760.

CHAPTER

15

The Cradle of the Revolution

J EFFERY AMHERST, THOUGH HE was knighted soon after
the taking of Montreal, and a few years later was raised to the
peerage as a baron, soon was forgotten at home.[50] It was
not so in America, where he had made a good impression.
Aside from the college, there are towns or cities named after
him in Massachusetts, Virginia, Maine, New Hampshire,
Pennsylvania, Ohio, Wisconsin, Minnesota, Kansas, and Nova
Scotia; and there is also an Amherstburg in Ontario.

He did not get killed in the field, for he was too sensible
to expose himself, and he didn't quote Gray. But he got a lot
done.

He made an excellent administrator, as might have been
expected. He divided Canada into three districts, centered
by Montreal, Trois Rivières, and Quebec, and he put a
brigadier in charge of each. He immediately began to pull
strings for his own recall, and Mr. Pitt promised him that
he would not be obliged to stay in America "a single day"
longer than was absolutely necessary. In fact, it was five years
from the time that he had landed at Louisbourg before he
could get back to his Kentish manor house, which he named
"Montreal."

He was the first military governor of British Canada, in the nature of things, but he was soon succeeded by General Murray, who, together with *his* successor, Guy Carleton, did an excellent, evenhanded job.

There was much for the General to do elsewhere, and soon he was back in New York City, where that same little stone house on the Battery once again served as his headquarters, though he often had to be in Albany as well. When as a reward for his services he was made a Knight Companion of the Bath, the ceremony was held, unaccountably, on Staten Island.

King George II, a small, disagreeable man, had dropped dead unexpectedly in his bedroom one morning before breakfast, just after the fall of Montreal, and his successor, his grandson, the young man who was George III, had the rather quaint idea that *he* and not Mr. Pitt should run Great Britain. However, he was starting slowly. Pitt was still in command. He had not yet been kicked upstairs to the House of Lords.

Mr. Pitt was by no means satisfied with the land he had grabbed. He wanted more, and Amherst got his instructions to seize all available French West Indian islands. The troops for this purpose were sent by him, or else were routed through him: they were under his command, though he did not take the field in person.

When Great Britain declared war on Spain, in 1763, the General was instructed to organize still another grand expedition, this one to take Havana. It was a bitter, nasty business, but successful.

One of the General's chief duties was to get the seacoast colonies to keep raising fresh bodies of militia, to maintain these at at least two-thirds and if possible three-quarters of their previous wartime strength, so that they could take over routine guard duties, releasing regulars for service in the Caribbean area. The colonies were not interested. They were sick of war, and now that France had been removed from the north and was no longer a danger to their frontier they saw no reason why they should go on soldiering.

The colonists—at least the New Englanders and those from the middle colonies—had another good reason to dislike the shifting of the war from Canada to the Caribbean. They had built a lucrative trade with the French West Indies where, because of the British Navy and also because the cognac interests in Paris had succeeded in sharply limiting the import into France of West Indian rum and the molasses with which to make it, the planters were desperate. The planters needed food in order to keep all those slaves alive, and the Yankees could provide food and would accept molasses in payment.

That the Yankees were dealing with the enemy made no difference to them. That the English, incensed, tried to stamp out the trade *did* make a difference.

It was the beginning of the bitterness that was to culminate in the American Revolution.

Amherst undoubtedly knew about this illegal trade, but except when it actively interfered with his own provisioning arrangements, the supplying of his own troops, he tolerated it.

Amherst's blind spot, an important one, was the Indians. He could not approve the methods of his principal Indian agent, Sir William Johnson, who wanted to keep the Iroquois quiet with pretty gifts and plenty of rum. Amherst made him grants for this purpose just at first, but only under protest, and he was soon to cease the practice. He didn't think that it was right to shower the savages with inducements in the form of trinkets and ribbons and mirrors and medals. He didn't think that it was dignified. The Indians should not be bribed to be good. If they misbehaved they should be punished, promptly and severely.

To this Sir William replied that a few thousand pounds spent on glass beads now might save many thousands in destroyed property later. The General had no patience with such talk.

Sir William might have pointed out that the gift method

was the one employed by the French, who, except in the case of the Iroquois, had been remarkably successful in their dealings with the redskins.

The Indians themselves were prompt to notice the difference in treatment. The French had mixed with them, laughed and cried with them. The English treated them like children—naughty children. The English seemed to think that they should be seen but not heard, and preferably not even seen most of the time. The wilderness fort until a little while earlier had been a gathering place, a place for a handout, perhaps even for a drinking party. These forts, which were also trading posts, were held by British soldiers now, and it was made clear to the red man that he wasn't wanted there—unless he had something to sell.

It was not this spirit, though it helped, that brought about rebellion. Rather, the savages soon saw that what the French had predicted was coming to pass. The new masters were land-hungry. Gradually, inexorably, they were pushing the Indians out of their best hunting grounds, their very livelihood. They were not passers-through; they were there to stay.

Even so, it is not likely that there would have been an uprising of the redskins if there had not happened to be a genius among them. Pontiac was an Ottawa chief (though his mother was an Ojibway) who not only could get men together but could keep them together, something that no other Indian ever had been known to do. The race had no talent for acting in concert. Before Pontiac it had never stayed with anything. But Pontiac, like Amherst, was a natural organizer.

The result of his exhortations is known in history as Pontiac's Conspiracy, a name that belittles it. For it was a war, and an exceptionally dirty war, marked by some of the most hideous torture sessions on record. Though much of it was bushfighting, guerrilla fighting, there were some sieges

Fire-rafts in the Detroit River during Pontiac's Conspiracy

—Detroit, Fort Pitt—that the Indians, previously hit-and-run warriors, kept up for weeks on end. Pontiac never did accomplish anything for his people, though he had a legitimate grievance; and eventually he was murdered, while drunk, by one of his own braves, and the whole thing fizzled out. It was estimated to have cost £100,000. The government could have bought a lot of beads for that.

Pontiac's Conspiracy, despite Pontiac's own personality and organizing ability, probably never would have taken place if the Indians had not been led to believe that France was about to reinvade Canada. When they learned that they could not count upon this, they lost interest.

Such was Pontiac's influence that he even got into his war one of the Iroquois tribes, the Senecas—the westernmost of the Six Nations and hence geographically the farthest from Sir William Johnson, whose mansion was near the mouth of the Mohawk.

In truth, and despite certain missionaries and *coureurs de bois*, France, exhausted, had no thought of trying an immediate reentry of America. Even while Pontiac's war was at its hottest the treaty of peace was signed, the Treaty of Paris.

This was done February 10, 1763. It had been preceded, in England, by a long and acrimonious newspaper discussion about the advisability or inadvisability of taking over such a vast wild section of the world as New France. There were those who favored the keeping of Guadeloupe instead. The Royal Navy had captured this West Indian island from the French while Wolfe was besieging Quebec, and there were many in the British Parliament, where the "sugar aristocracy" was riding high, who would have preferred Guadeloupe and who urged its annexation and the abandonment of Canada. After all, they pointed out, sugar prices were high, the demand was great and growing, and Guadeloupe was rich. What was Canada? Nothing but a vast frozen waste, which produced only furs. Nevertheless the diplomats decided upon Canada.

What would have happened if they voted the other way it might be hard to imagine. For the Atlantic seaboard colonies, especially the northern and middle ones, would still be faced with the threat of French-Indian raids. As it was, freed of this threat—for the frontier had been forced back, the mountains crossed—they did not see any need to have redcoats quartered upon them, nor did they feel inclined to pay the extra taxes that the British at home would be obliged to pay if the nation, what with the staggering costs of the war, was to avert bankruptcy.

The British had got a great deal of the world as a result of the war just finished, but they had got at the same time the biggest national debt known to history—£130,000,000. The interest alone (it varied) was between £4,500,000 and £5,000,000 a year. Obviously something must be done.

It was no coincidence that so many of the general officers on the colonial side in the American Revolution had got their military training in the French and Indian War—Washington, Stark, Putnam, Pomeroy, to name but a few—for that war led directly and inevitably to the Revolution. It was then that America learned how to fight.

Notes

1. The French camp was near the present site of Farmington, Pa. Under her charter of June 2, 1609, Virginia at that time claimed all of what is now western Pennsylvania, West Virginia, Kentucky, Ohio, Indiana, Illinois, Michigan, and Wisconsin.

2. There is even a case of record of a New York militiaman at the time of the siege of Fort Oswego in August, 1756, passing out, drunk, at the edge of the surrounding forest, to wake in the morning, having remembered nothing, without his hair. *He* survived.

3. *Writings*, I, 70.

4. He was an Iroquois of *some* sort, long before the taking-in of the Tuscaroras, and most of the myths have him a Mohawk. Henry Wadsworth Longfellow unaccountably seemed to think that he had been a Chippewa.

5. "Canada lived by the fur trade and for this required free range and indefinite space. In the English colonies agriculture played an important part. This could be carried out in limited areas and there was therefore no present need to cross the forest-covered Alleghenies. The tendency of the English was, therefore, to take firm root before they spread,

while the French shot offshoots far out and quickly into the wilderness. The French colonists were the more military by training and tradition; they were quicker in recognizing strategic points which were seized and held by armed force, forming no agricultural basis, but attracting the Indians by trade and holding them by conversion." Whitton, 43.

6. It is noteworthy that when railroads were built these same openings were used. The New York Central uses the Mohawk Valley, the Pennsylvania the Susquehanna River Valley, and the Baltimore and Ohio the valley of the Potomac and Cumberland Gap.

7. Properly, he was the lieutenant governor, but he did all the work. The real governor was Lord Albemarle, who sat in London and accepted a princely salary, half of which he sent on to Dinwiddie. This was a well-established custom of the time. It extended to the military in England, though not in the American colonies. A British army colonel seldom mounted epaulets or strapped on a sword, much less reviewed his regiment, *much* less took the field. These duties were left to the lieutenant colonels.

8. A letter to Governor Dinwiddie, June 3: "We have just finish'd a small palisado'd Fort, in which, with my small numbers, I shall not fear the attack of 500 men." *Writings,* I, 73.

9. This has been restored by the National Park Service and is open to the public. It is on U.S. Route 40 near Uniontown, Fayette County, Pennsylvania.

10. The house still stands. It is a museum now.

11. Van Doren, *Benjamin Franklin,* 220.

12. So respectable a military authority as Sir John Fortescue thought that the Philadelphia route would have been better. *History of the British Army,* II, 270.

13. Franklin, *Autobiography,* 151.

14. This is the same man who twenty years later as Lieutenant General Gage, commander in chief of all His

Majesty's military forces in America, ordered the raid on the stores collected at Concord and so precipitated the Revolution.

15. "Braddock would not have been ashamed to have organized such a march in Flanders or to have made it while even His Royal Highness, the Duke of Cumberland, was observing it." Freeman, *George Washington*, II, 67–68.

16. "Whereas in New France there was a unified Indian policy, with the Governor General speaking to the natives in the name of all Frenchmen, this was not true of England overseas, in spite of the efforts of those at the Albany Congress to lend an air of unanimity in the presence of representatives of the Iroquoian Confederation. As a consequence, in this first contest between the French and the English in the new war now commencing, the French were able to rely not only upon the support of their Canadian Indians but even on that of their late enemies the Mingos, the Shawnee, and the Delawares, who now came over to them and sought to harass Washington's retreating army, left without any Indian support." Gipson, *British Empire*, VI, 45.

17. It is only fair to point out, as Hamilton does in his admirable *The French and Indian Wars* (p. 158), that these two regiments, by no means the pride of the British Army to begin with, had been "fleshed out" in England by means of drafts upon other regiments. No colonel, obliged to give up so-and-so-many of his men, would surrender the good ones. Rather, being human, he would give up the misfits, the weaklings. In addition, when the regiments got to America they enlisted 200-odd apiece, and these were raw recruits who were allowed only a few months of training. In other words, the 44th and 48th at the time of the disaster on the banks of the Monongahela contained only somewhat less than half out-and-out, honest-to-goodness British regulars. It was astonishing, in the circumstances, that they did as well as they did.

18. Washington, *Writings,* I, 151.

19. The title might have been an assumed one. It was a custom of the time in the French Army and the various German armies, though not in the British Army, to give all officers, even subalterns, *some* kind of title: the assumption was that every officer was a nobleman, or at least was entitled to be treated as one. Professional soldiers took to these titles as a matter of course, and with no thought to deceive. Thus, in the American Revolution Baron de Kalb was not a baron at all and did not even rate the "de," while Baron von Steuben, who did not rate the "von," was not a baron either. However, Count Pulaski was a sure-enough count, as the Marquis de Lafayette was indeed a marquis. Von Dieskau had been born in Germany but the title can be assumed to be French—and honorary.

20. Williams College was to be named after him.

21. One is tempted both to anticipate and to paraphrase General Pierre Bosquet when he had watched the charge of the Light Brigade at Balaklava: *"C'était magnifique, mais ce n'était pas la guerre."*

22. "Louisbourg was the most thoroughly hated place in all America." Wood, *Great Fortress,* 74.

23. "Unhappily for these exiles, the accumulated afflictions that came upon them were, one must affirm, largely self-inflicted. Whenever it was open for them to choose between a wise and an unwise course of action, they had consistently chosen the latter—doubtless as a result of bad advice." Gipson, *British Empire,* VI, 315.

24. "No general in England or on Continental service wielded the power which the commander in chief in America possessed. Slow as the process may have been, in the end every department, with certain definitely named limitations, transferred its authority in America to Loudoun. He issued all warrants for the payment of money; he authorized the issuing of arms and stores from the Ordnance Office in Amer-

ica; he appointed officers to every vacancy except that of colonel; he reviewed court-martial findings; he supervised the superintendency of Indian affairs; and he gave orders to the naval officers on the interior lakes. He was therefore the representative for military affairs in America of the king, the Ordnance Board, the War Office, the Treasury, and to some extent the Admiralty. He was England's military government extended to the colonies." Pargellis, *Lord Loudoun,* 79–80.

25. The Seven Years' War was "a murderous, sordid affair, born of an international bar room fight, land-grabbing greed and fomented, whipped-up jealousies." Murray, *Decisive Battles,* 500–501.

26. The college song, otherwise admirable, is inaccurate in the matter of its hero's title. Amherst was not even a baronet, not even a knight, when he crossed the sea in 1758. He was not knighted until 1771, and not created a baron until 1776. It was as *Lord* Amherst that he was to decline the overall leadership of the British forces in the American Revolution, though he did consent to act in an advisory capacity at home.

27. Waugh, *James Wolfe,* 182–83.

28. Mayo, *Jeffery Amherst,* 108; Whitton, *Wolfe and North America,* 220.

29. "The second siege of Louisbourg was a straightforward European operation that happened to be waged on the soil of North America, but conceded nothing to those special conditions of this continent which in most cases limited the action that could be taken." Hamilton, *The French and Indian Wars,* 230.

30. *Letters,* IV, 36.

31. Fortescue, *British Army,* II, 321.

32. That is, if we except the force with which Montezuma met the little army of Cortes. Its exact size is not known, though it was always described as very large.

33. The citizens of the Massachusetts Bay Colony thought so highly of Lord Howe that they gave the British government £250 in tax money for the erection of a memorial in Westminster Abbey, where you may still see it. There were ever to be those who would say that if Howe had lived there would not have been an American Revolution; but this is going somewhat too far.

34. Now Kingston, Ontario.

35. The present city of Rome, N.Y.

36. He was to die a major general in New York just before the Revolution.

37. It was at this camp that a British Army surgeon, Dr. Shuckburg, amused by the yokels who still came swarming in from the countryside to gawp at the soldiers in the camp, wrote new words to an old marching song that came to be known as "Yankee Doodle." The song until this time had been generally known as "Lydia Locket."

> "Lydia Locket lost her pocket,
> Kitty Fisher found it.
> Not a bit of money in it,
> Only binding round it."

This, which doesn't make any sense today, was highly popular in its own time. Lydia Locket and Kitty Fisher were loose ladies of London, and doubtless the meaning that has been lost was a bawdy one.

An earlier version goes all the way back to Oliver Cromwell's time:

> "Nankee Doodle came to town
> Upon a little pony;
> He stuck a feather in his hat
> And called it macaroni."

Oscar George Theodore Sonneck, *Report on "The Star-Spangled Banner," "Hail Columbia," "America," "Yankee Doodle"* (Washington: Government Printing Office, 1909).

Also *Yankee Doodle-Doo, A Collection of Songs of the Early American State*, compiled and with an introduction and notes by Grenville Vernon (New York: Payson & Clark, Ltd., 1927).

38. It is generally believed that the French gave their stronghold this name because the sound of the raceway between Lake George and Lake Champlain made them think of chimes. As for the name Ticonderoga, this was reported to be Iroquoian for "great noise," or something to that effect. It could be. It was at this very spot, 160 years before, that Champlain inadvisedly turned his muskets on the Mohawks, who thus heard firearms for the first time. Thanks to members of the Pell family, the place still stands and has been restored. It is a museum operated by the Fort Ticonderoga Association, a nonprofit educational organization.

39. "More nonsense has been written about the fortifications of Quebec than on almost any other subject in modern history." Stacey, *Quebec, 1759*, 28. This, one of the latest, is also one of the best of the many books about the siege of Quebec. Parkman's *Montcalm and Wolfe*, however, remains the most readable.

40. Bougainville after the war was to explore the South Sea islands, discovering many of them, bringing back many botanical specimens, among them being the climbing vine with the beautiful flowers named after him. It is notable that down among the British supply ships on the St. Lawrence one was skippered by Lieutenant James Cook, Royal Navy reservist, who was to attain even greater fame as a Pacific explorer and discoverer. They never met.

41. Waugh, *James Wolfe*, 115.

42. "The English say that the storm saved the French; the French, with as much reason, that it saved the English." Parkman, *Montcalm and Wolfe*, II, 74.

43. Now called Wolfe's Cove. Ocean liners tie up there.

44. Millions still believe the story that the Highlander,

asked what regiment his was, replied without hesitation "De la Reine," and that the sentry asked no more. In fact, the Régiment de la Reine at that time was serving under Bourlamaque at Ile aux Noix. Also, as Stacey points out (*Quebec, 1759*, 124), "In any case, no French sentry would have asked such a question. Transport was no task for the regular regiments, and the men in charge of the boats would have been militiamen, the best people for the job."

45. William Howe, who was to be so prominent in the American Revolution a little later, did not inherit the title. A middle brother, Admiral Richard ("Black Dick") Howe, became the viscount. William Howe was not to get the title until much later, when his seagoing brother died. By that time he had been knighted for his capture of New York City.

46. There were probably only four men with him at the time, for it had not been noted that he fell. Benjamin West's famous picture of this scene shows scores of anxious attendants, a big occasion. It was not that the painter did not know better: he was only following the conventions of the day.

47. Until this time he had scraped along on an estate income of £800 inherited, besides the income from two regiments that he "owned"—the 15th, bringing in £600 a year, and the 60th, bringing in £200. Mayo, *Jeffery Amherst*, 246.

48. "The plan was delicate in the extreme and called for the greatest nicety of calculation, for the three armies must start from three different points hundreds of miles apart without possibility of inter-communication, and yet arrive at their goal together, lest the French should concentrate and overwhelm Murray's or Haviland's corps in detail." Fortescue, *History of the British Army*, II, 402.

49. Admiral Corbett found it "one of the most perfect and astonishing bits of work which the annals of British warfare can show." *Seven Years' War*, II, 117.

50. "Amherst to the majority of Englishmen is but a name: as though it were a small thing for a colonel, taken

straight from the classic fields of Flanders, to cross the Atlantic to a savage wilderness, assume command of disheartened troops and the direction of discordant colonists, and quietly and deliberately to organize victory. He was the greatest military administrator produced by England since the death of Marlborough, and remained the greatest until the rise of Wellington." Fortescue, *History of the British Army*, II, 411.

Glossary of Eighteenth-Century Military Terms

ABATIS. A roadblock that was made of chopped-down trees piled on top of one another, the branches toward the oncoming or expected enemy.

BARBETTE. A wooden or earthen platform inside a fortification, on which the cannons were placed in order to allow them to shoot over the rampart.

BASTION. A projecting masonry work, usually V-shaped, on the wall of a fort, outside. From it, attackers along the CURTAIN could be cross-fired.

BLUNDERBUSS. A short chunky weapon, a musket, featured by a huge bell-shaped muzzle. The blunderbuss could discharge a lethal shower of stones, nails, lead slugs, what-have-you—but only for a short distance. Despite the popular picture, it seems certain that none of the Pilgrim Fathers carried blunderbusses. Why should they? The blunderbuss was no good as a bird gun, and any reasonably nimble Indian could hurl his tomahawk ten times the distance that a blunderbuss would carry. The blunderbuss was good only at close quarters, where its enormous muzzle had a frightening effect. It was favored by the drivers of stagecoaches and by householders who had some cause to expect burglars. It was never, properly, a military weapon, though it might sometimes be used, *ad terrorum,* in hit-and-run raids.

BROWN BESS was the nickname of a musket introduced into the British Army in 1682 and which, with minor modifications, continued to be the official arm until 1842. It was, for the time, unexpectedly short and light; and it was efficient. That it was not accurate did not trouble war-makers, who placed all emphasis upon controlled mass fire rather than upon marksmanship. It could be reloaded very quickly. The gun had a naturally brown walnut stock, while its barrels and other metal parts had been artificially browned with acid: hence the name.

CANISTER was a canvas or cloth bag filled with small round lead or iron pellets and crammed into a cannon on top of a charge of gunpowder. It would not carry as far as solid shot, but it was deadly at close quarters.

CARCASS. Nothing to do with a cadaver. It was a metal can punched with holes and filled with oiled rags that were set ablaze when the carcass was shot from a cannon. The purpose, of course, was to cause a building or a whole town to catch fire. During the Revolution, carcasses were used from warships in the Battle of Bunker Hill to destroy the deserted village of Charlestown, which in the beginning had harbored snipers. It was not very effective in that particular brush, and Marines had to be landed with old-fashioned torches to finish the job.

CASE SHOT. Another name for CANISTER.

COHORN was one of the few words in the military vocabulary of the time that was not French. It, and the weapon—a small stubby howitzer—were originally Dutch: *coehoorn.*

COUNTERSCARP. The outer wall or slope of the ditch surrounding a fort. The inner wall was the SCARP.

CHEVAUX-DE-FRISE. A crisscross of heavy timbers, usually tipped with steel spikes, calculated to stop infantry. Sometimes, however, this was used underwater in an effort to prevent ships from passing a certain point.

CURTAIN. The wall of a fortification between BASTION, towers, or other crossfire projections.

DEMILUNES were half-moon-shaped outworks, not large.

EMBRASURE. An opening in a PARAPET through which a cannon is fired.

EPAULEMENT. The "shoulder" of a fort wall; the place where the CURTAIN and BASTION meet.

FASCINES were bundles of twigs and sticks hastily assembled and tied together. They were used for constructing gun platforms and, even more, for filling ditches to permit the passage of military vehicles. From such a bundle, the symbol of ancient Rome, came the name of the late unlamented fascists.

FEU DE JOIE. This was a musket salute performed by two double files, every other man firing the first time, the rest the second time on the way back. It was a complicated business.

FLANK COMPANIES. In each British infantry regiment there were a company of grenadiers (who no longer carried grenades) and a company of so-called light infantry, and these were traditionally placed upon the flanks. They were elite troops. When there was an especially dangerous or delicate mission to perform, the flank companies were pulled out of various regiments.

FLÈCHE. A small defensive ditch, unroofed, in the shape of an arrowhead, the point toward the expected enemy. (The word means "arrow" in French.) It was an outwork, a deterrent, a stopgap, not a real fortlet.

GABIONS were baskets made of any material, wicker being preferred, and filled with earth and stones. Clumsy, heavy things, they were used for shoring up parapets, filling ditches, protecting field guns. They were the eighteenth-century equivalent of sandbags.

GRAPE or GRAPESHOT was similar to CANISTER except that the balls were smaller and there were more of them.

HOWITZER meant then exactly what it does today: a smallish cannon sharply uptilted, used, mostly in mountain warfare, to lob shells or balls into a protected position.

MATROSS. A sort of assistant artilleryman who helped to handle a fieldpiece in action. He was a regular member of the army, not like the horse drivers who, in both armies, were hired civilians and who retired when the guns began to boom—if not sooner.

MORTAR. Just what it is now—a short large-calibered piece of ordnance so trunnioned that it can shoot very high.

PARAPET. The wall of a fortification.

PICKET. A small party of foot soldiers sent forth in advance of the army to feel out the enemy and harass him if he approaches.

POUNDAGE. Field guns, whether on ship or ashore, were rated by the weight of the balls they could fire, which were reckoned in pounds avoirdupois. Thus, four-pounder, six-pounder, etc. This applied only to solid ball, not to CANISTER or GRAPE or CARCASSES.

RAMPART. Parapet.

RAVELIN. This was a small earthwork, an outwork, with only two faces, something like a FLÈCHE.

REDAN. It would take an expert to distinguish this from a RAVELIN, though it might be somewhat smaller.

REDOUBT. This was larger and stronger. It might be a square or some other multiangled shape, but it was always completely enclosed, never open at one end.

SAUCISSON. This, in French, means a large or German-type sausage. In eighteenth-century armies it meant a large FASCINE of roughly that shape.

SPONTOON. This was a sort of halberd or pike carried by sergeants on both sides, for protection purposes, when battle was expected. Often too these were carried by officers, whose tooth-picky swords could scarely be expected to prevail against an infantryman with a six-foot musket *and* bayonet.

TENAILLE. A small, low fortification, sometimes with only one entrance, sometimes with two, occasionally roofed, placed for annoyance purposes outside the CURTAIN between two BASTIONS.

UP IN THE AIR. An unprotected flank was said to have been left "up in the air."

Bibliography

ADAMS, HERBERT BAXTER. "Lord Amherst." *New England Magazine,* February, 1896.

ALBERTS, ROBERT C. *The Most Extraordinary Adventures of Major Robert Strobo.* Boston: Houghton Mifflin Company, 1965.

ALDEN, JOHN RICHARD. *General Gage in America.* Baton Rouge: Louisiana State University Press, 1948.

ALVORD, CLARENCE WALWORTH, and CARTER, CLARENCE EDWIN, editors. *The Critical Period, 1763–1765.* Springfield: Illinois State Historical Library, 1915.

AMBLER, CHARLES H. *George Washington and the West.* Chapel Hill: University of North Carolina Press, 1936.

ANDREWS, CHARLES M. *The Colonial Background of the American Revolution.* New Haven: Yale University Press, 1923.

———. *The Colonial Period of American History.* 4 vols. New Haven: Yale University Press, 1967.

BAKER-CROTHERS, HAYES. *Virginia and the French and Indian War.* Chicago: University of Chicago Press, 1928.

164

BANCROFT, GEORGE. *History of the United States of America.* 6 vols. New York: D. Appleton and Company, 1883.

BAXTER, JAMES P. "What Caused the Deportation of the Acadians?" American Antiquarian Society *Proceedings,* New Series, Vol. XIII.

BEER, GEORGE LOUIS. *British Colonial Policy, 1754–1765.* New York: The Macmillan Company, 1907.

——. *The Commercial Policy of England Toward the American Colonies.* New York: Columbia University Press, 1893.

BIRD, HARRISON. *Battle for a Continent.* New York: Oxford University Press, 1965.

——. *Navies in the Mountains: The Battles on the Waters of Lake Champlain and Lake George, 1609–1814.* New York: Oxford University Press, 1962.

BOORSTIN, DANIEL J. *The Americans: The Colonial Experience.* New York: Random House, Inc., 1958.

BRADLEY, ARTHUR GRANVILLE. *The Fight with France for North America.* New York: E. P. Dutton and Co., 1902.

BUCK, PHILIP W. *The Politics of Mercantilism.* New York: Henry Holt and Company, 1942.

CARTER, CLARENCE EDWIN, *see* ALVORD, CLARENCE WALWORTH.

CHANNING, EDWARD. *A History of the United States.* 6 vols. New York: The Macmillan Company, 1905–1925.

CHARTERIS, EVAN. *William Augustus Duke of Cumberland and the Seven Years' War.* London: Hutchinson & Co., 1927.

CLELAND, HUGH. *George Washington in the Ohio Valley.* Pittsburgh: University of Pittsburgh Press, 1955.

CORBETT, SIR JULIAN S. *England in the Seven Years' War: A Study in Combined Strategy.* 2 vols. London: Longmans, Green & Co., 1918.

COUPLAND, REGINALD. *The Quebec Act: A Study in Statesmanship.* Oxford: The Clarendon Press, 1925.

CREASY, SIR EDWARD S. *Fifteen Decisive Battles of the World.* Edited, with nine new chapters, by Robert Hammond Murray. Harrisburg, Pa.: The Military Service Publishing Co., 1944.

CUNEO, JOHN R. *Robert Rogers of the Rangers.* New York: Oxford University Press, 1959.

DE FOREST, LOUIS E., *see* POMEROY, SETH.

DE FOREST, LOUIS EFFINGHAM, editor. *Louisbourg Journals 1745.* New York: Society of Colonial Wars in the State of New York, 1932.

DICKERSON, OLIVER MORTON. *American Colonial Government, 1696–1765: A Study of the British Board of Trade in Its Relation to the American Colonies, Political, Industrial, Administrative.* Cleveland, Ohio: The Arthur H. Clark Company, 1912.

DOUGHTY, ARTHUR G. *The Acadian Exiles.* Toronto: Glasgow, Brook & Company, 1920.

————. *The Cradle of New France: A Story of the City Founded by Champlain.* Montreal: The Cambridge Corporation, Ltd., 1908.

DOUGHTY, ARTHUR G., *see* KNOX, CAPT. JOHN.

DOUGHTY, ARTHUR G., and PARMELEE, G. W. *The Siege of Quebec and the Battle of the Plains of Abraham.* 6 vols. Quebec: Dussault and Proulx, 1901.

DOWNEY, FAIRFAX. *Louisbourg: Key to a Continent.* Englewood Cliffs, N.J.: Prentice-Hall, Inc., 1965.

DRAKE, SAMUEL G. *The Five Years French and Indian War (1744–1749).* Boston: Samuel G. Drake, 1870.

EDMONDS, WALTER D. *The Musket and the Cross: The Struggle of France and England for North America.* Boston: Little, Brown and Company, 1968.

ELDON, CARL WILLIAM. *England's Subsidy Policy Towards the Colonies During the Seven Years' War.* Philadelphia: University of Pennsylvania Press, 1938.

FALKNER, LEONARD. *Forge of Liberty.* New York: E. P. Dutton and Co., Inc., 1959.

FISK, JOHN. *New France and New England.* Boston: Houghton Mifflin Company, 1902.

FITZPATRICK, JOHN CLEMENT, *see* WASHINGTON, GEORGE.

FLEXNER, JAMES THOMAS. *George Washington: The Forge of Experience (1732–1775).* Boston: Little, Brown and Company, 1965.

————. *Mohawk Baronet: Sir William Johnson of New York.* New York: Harper & Row, 1959.

FORTESCUE, JOHN W. *History of the British Army.* 10 vols. New York: The Macmillan Company, 1899–1920.

FRANKLIN, BENJAMIN. *The Autobiography of Benjamin Franklin.* Edited by Nathan G. Goodman. New York: The Modern Library, 1932.

FREEMAN, DOUGLAS SOUTHALL. *George Washington: A Biography.* 6 vols. New York: Charles Scribner's Sons, 1948–1954.

FULLER, J. F. C. *Decisive Battles: Their Influence upon History and Civilization.* New York: Charles Scribner's Sons, 1940.

GIPSON, LAWRENCE HENRY. *The Coming of the American Revolution, 1763–1775.* New York: Harper & Brothers, 1954.

————. *The British Empire Before the American Revolution.* 9 vols. New York: Alfred A. Knopf, 1958–1967.

GOODMAN, NATHAN G., *see* FRANKLIN, BENJAMIN.

HAMILTON, CHARLES, editor. *Braddock's Defeat: The Journal of Captain Robert Cholmley's Batman; The Journal of a British Officer; Halkett's Orderly Book.* Norman: University of Oklahoma Press, 1959.

HAMILTON, EDWARD P. *Fort Ticonderoga: Key to a Continent.* Boston: Little, Brown and Company, 1964.

———. *The French and Indian Wars.* Garden City: Doubleday & Company, 1962.

HECKSCHER, ELI F. *Mercantilism.* Translated from the Swedish by Mendel Shapiro. London: G. Allan & Unwin, Ltd., 1935.

HIBBERT, CHRISTOPHER. *Wolfe at Quebec.* Cleveland, Ohio: The World Publishing Company, 1959.

HORROCKS, JOHN WESLEY. *A Short History of Mercantilism.* London: Methuen & Co., 1925.

HULBERT, ARCHER BUTLER. *Braddock's Road, and Three Relative Papers.* Cleveland, Ohio: The Arthur H. Clark Company, 1903.

———. *The Old Glade (Forbes's) Road.* Cleveland, Ohio: The Arthur H. Clark Company, 1903.

———. *Washington and the West.* New York: The Century Company, 1905.

———. *Washington's Road (Nemacolin's Path).* Cleveland, Ohio: The Arthur H. Clark Company, 1903.

HUTCHINSON, THOMAS. *History of the Province of Massachusetts Bay.* 3 vols. London, 1828.

JOHNSON, WILLIAM. *Papers of Sir William Johnson,* edited by James Sullivan. 14 vols. Albany: The University of the State of New York, 1921.

KINGSFORD, WILLIAM. *The History of Canada.* 8 vols. Toronto: Rowsell & Hutchinson, 1892–1893.

KIRKE, HENRY. *The First English Conquest of Canada*. London: S. Low, Marston and Co., Ltd., 1908.

————. *The Virginia Frontier, 1754–1763*. Baltimore: The Johns Hopkins Press, 1925.

KNOLLENBERG, BERNHARD. *George Washington: The Virginia Period, 1732–1775*. Durham, N.C.: Duke University Press, 1964.

————. *Origin of the American Revolution, 1759–1766*. New York: The Macmillan Company, 1960.

KNOX, CAPT. JOHN. *An historical journal of the campaigns in North America for the years 1757, 1758, 1759, and 1760*. Edited by Arthur G. Doughty. 3 vols. Toronto: The Champlain Society, 1914–1916.

KOONTZ, LOUIS KNOTT. *Robert Dinwiddie, His Career in American Colonial Government and Westward Expansion*. Glendale, Calif.: The Arthur H. Clark Company, 1941.

LABAREE, LEONARD W. *Royal Government in America: A Study of the British Colonial System Before 1783*. New York: Frederick Ungar Publishing Company, 1958.

LECKY, W. E. H. *History of England in the Eighteenth Century*. 8 vols. London: Longmans, Green & Company, 1878–1890.

LONG, J. C. *Lord Jeffery Amherst, a Soldier of the King*. New York: The Macmillan Company, 1933.

McCARDELL, LEE. *Ill-Starred General: Braddock of the Coldstream Guards*. Pittsburgh: University of Pittsburgh Press, 1958.

McLENNAN, J. S. *Louisbourg, from Its Foundation to Its Fall, 1713–1758*. London: Macmillan and Co., Ltd., 1911.

MAYO, LAWRENCE SHAW. *Jeffery Amherst, a Biography*. New York: Longmans, Green and Co., 1916.

MILLER, JOHN C. *Origins of the American Revolution.* Boston: Little, Brown and Company, 1948.

MORRIS, RICHARD B. *Government and Labor in Early America.* New York: Columbia University Press, 1946.

MURRAY, ROBERT HAMMOND, *see* CREASY, SIR EDWARD S.

O'CALLAGHAN, E. B., editor. *The Documentary History of the State of New-York.* 4 vols. Albany: Weed, Parsons & Co., 1850–1851.

O'MEARA, WALTER. *Guns at the Forks: The Story of Fort Duquesne and Fort Pitt in the Wilderness War Between France and England for the Ownership of a Continent.* Englewood Cliffs, N.J.: Prentice-Hall, Inc., 1965.

OSGOOD, HERBERT L. *The American Colonies in the Eighteenth Century.* 3 vols. New York: Columbia University Press, 1924.

PARES, RICHARD. *Merchants and Planters.* Cambridge: Cambridge University Press, 1960.

―――. *Yankees and Creoles: The Trade Between North America and the West Indies Before the American Revolution.* Cambridge: Harvard University Press, 1952.

PARGELLIS, STANLEY. "Braddock's Defeat." *American Historical Review,* XLI, pp. 253–269.

―――. *Lord Loudoun in North America.* New Haven: Yale University Press, 1933.

―――, editor. *Military Affairs in North America, 1748–1765: Selected Documents from the Cumberland Papers in Windsor Castle.* New York: D. Appleton-Century Company, 1936.

PARKMAN, FRANCIS. *Montcalm and Wolfe: France and England in North America.* 3 vols. Boston: Little, Brown and Co., 1897.

PARMELEE, G. W., *see* DOUGHTY, ARTHUR G.

PECKHAM, HOWARD H. *The Colonial Wars, 1689–1762.* Chicago: University of Chicago Press, 1964.

PEPPERRELL, SIR WILLIAM. "Journal." American Antiquarian Society *Proceedings*, 1911.

POMEROY, SETH. *The Journals and Papers of Seth Pomeroy*, edited by Louis E. De Forest. New Haven, Conn.: Society of Colonial Wars in the State of New York, 1926.

REED, VICTORIA. "Sir William Pepperrell and the Capture of Louisbourg." *New England Magazine*, June, 1895.

RIKER, THAD W. "The Politics Behind Braddock's Expedition." *American Historical Review*, Vol. XIII, 1907–1908, pp. 742–752.

ROGERS, ROBERT. *Journal of Major Robert Rogers*. Ann Arbor, Mich.: University Microfilms, Inc., 1966.

ROSSITER, CLINTON. *Seedtime of the Republic: The Origin of the American Tradition of Political Liberty*. New York: Harcourt, Brace and Co., 1953.

SARGENT, WINTHROP. *The History of an Expedition Against Fort Du Quesne*. Philadelphia: Lippincott, Grambo & Co., 1855.

SCHUTZ, JOHN A. *William Shirley, King's Governor of Massachusetts*. Chapel Hill: University of North Carolina Press, 1961.

SHAPIRO, MENDEL, *see* HECKSCHER, ELI F.

SHY, JOHN. *Toward Lexington: The Role of the British Army in the Coming of the American Revolution*. Princeton: Princeton University Press, 1965.

STACEY, C. P. *Quebec, 1759: The Siege and the Battle*. Toronto: The Macmillan Company of Canada, Ltd., 1959.

SULLIVAN, JAMES, *see* JOHNSON, WILLIAM.

SUTHERLAND, STELLA H. *Population Distribution in Colonial America*. New York: Columbia University Press, 1956.

SYLVESTER, HERBERT MILTON. *Indian Wars of New England*. 3 vols. Boston: W. B. Clarke Company, 1910.

TARBOX, INCREASE N. *Life of Israel Putnam ("Old Put")*. Boston: Lockwood, Brooks, and Co., 1876.

THWAITES, REUBEN GOLD. *France in America, 1497–1763*. New York: Harper & Brothers, 1905.

VAN DOREN, CARL. *Benjamin Franklin*. New York: The Viking Press, 1938.

VOORHEES, FELIX. *Acadian Reminiscences: The True Story of Evangeline*. New Orleans: E. P. Rivas, 1948.

WALPOLE, HORACE. *The Letters of Horace Walpole, Fourth Earl of Oxford*. 16 vols. Edited by Mrs. Paget Toynbee. Oxford: The Clarendon Press, 1904.

WASHINGTON, GEORGE. *The Writings of George Washington, from the Original Manuscript Sources, 1745–1799*. 39 vols. Edited by John Clement Fitzpatrick. Washington: U.S. Government Printing Office, 1931–1944.

WAUGH, W. T. *James Wolfe, Man and Soldier*. Montreal: Louis Carrier & Co., 1928.

WHITTON, F. E. *Wolfe and North America*. Boston: Little, Brown Company, 1929.

WILLIAMS, BASIL. *The Whig Supremacy, 1714–1760*. Oxford: The Clarendon Press, 1939.

WILLSON, BECKLES. *The Life and Letters of James Wolfe*. London: William Heinemann, 1909.

WOOD, WILLIAM. *The Great Fortress: A Chronicle of Louisbourg, 1720–1760*. Toronto: Glasgow, Brook & Company, 1915.

————. *The Passing of New France*. Toronto: Glasgow, Brook & Company, 1920.

WRONG, GEORGE M. *The Conquest of New France*. New Haven: Yale University Press, 1918.

————. *The Rise and Fall of New France*. 2 vols. New York: The Macmillan Company, 1928.

Index